JAMES

FAITH / WORKS

MATT CHANDLER

LifeWay Press®
Nashville, Tennessee

EDITORIAL TEAM
GROUPS MINISTRY PUBLISHING

Michael Kelley
Director, Groups Ministry

Brian Daniel
Manager, Short-Term Discipleship

Joel Polk
Editorial Team Leader

Jeremy Maxfield
Writer

Reid Patton
Content Editor

David Haney
Production Editor

Jon Rodda
Art Director

STUDENT MINISTRY PUBLISHING

Ben Trueblood
Director, Student Ministry

John Paul Basham
Manager, Student Ministry Publishing

Karen Daniel
Editorial Team Leader

Jeff Belcher
Content Editor

Stephanie Livengood
Content Specialist

Amy Lyon
Graphic Designer

Published by LifeWay Press®

ISBN 978-1-5359-0918-1 • Item 005804601

Dewey decimal classification: 227.91
Subject headings: BIBLE. N.T. JAMES—STUDY AND TEACHING \ FAITH \ CHRISTIAN LIFE

To order additional copies of this resource, write to LifeWay Resources Customer Service; One LifeWay Plaza; Nashville, TN 37234; fax 615-251-5933; phone toll free 800-458-2772; order online at LifeWay.com; email orderentry@lifeway.com; or visit the LifeWay Christian Store serving you.

Printed in the United States of America

Student Ministry Publishing
LifeWay Resources
One LifeWay Plaza
Nashville, TN 37234

CONTENTS

ABOUT THE AUTHOR

MATT CHANDLER serves as the lead pastor of teaching at The Village Church in the Dallas/Fort Worth metroplex. He came to The Village in December 2002 and describes his tenure as a replanting effort to change the theological and philosophical culture of the congregation. The church has witnessed a tremendous response, growing from 160 people to more than 11,000, including campuses in Flower Mound, Dallas, Plano, and Fort Worth.

Alongside his current role as lead pastor, Matt is involved in church-planting efforts both locally and internationally through The Village, as well as in various strategic partnerships. Prior to accepting the pastorate at The Village, Matt had a vibrant itinerant ministry for more than ten years that gave him the opportunity to speak to thousands of people in America and abroad about the glory of God and the beauty of Jesus.

Matt is the author of *Take Heart*; *To Live Is Christ, to Die Is Gain; Mingling of Souls; The Explicit Gospel* Bible study (LifeWay, 2012); and *The Apostles' Creed* Bible study (LifeWay, 2017). He's also a coauthor of *Creature of the Word* (LifeWay, 2012).

Other than knowing Jesus, Matt's greatest joy is being married to Lauren and being the dad to their three children: Audrey, Reid, and Norah.

INTRODUCTION

Faith works. This is the message of James. James shows that faith and works are not enemies but friends. Without faith, we could never find the strength to trust God. We would never be able to see above the trials we meet and keep our eyes focused on the King. We don't work to be saved; we work because we're saved. Without faith, our works are empty service. Without works, our faith is dead. Works reveal the genuineness of and enrich our faith.

To illustrate this tension, James compares the person who has faith but not works to the person who stares at his face in the mirror but then forgets the way he looks as soon as he turns away. But with faith that works, we stay on the journey of being sanctified, knowing we'll be perfected once we reach the other side.

The repeated cry of James is that faith apart from works can never be sustained. We should proclaim this truth because faith makes us doers of the Word, not just hearers. Faith keeps us humble, not proud; directs us to bless, not to curse; and causes us to show mercy, not judgment. Faith leads us to true religion that extends itself in favor toward others. Faith causes us to preach the good news to every tribe, tongue, and nation. Faith motivates us to worship our God for all eternity. This is the message of James: Faith works.

HOW TO USE

James: Faith/Works provides a guided process for individuals and small groups to walk through the New Testament Book of James. This Bible study book includes thirteen weeks of content, each divided into two major sections: "Group Study" and "Personal Study." A leader guide is also provided to prepare those who are leading groups through this journey.

GROUP STUDY

Regardless of the day of the week your group meets, each week of content begins with a group session. This group session is designed to last sixty minutes, with approximately twenty minutes dedicated to video teaching and another forty minutes to group discussion.

Each group study uses the following format to facilitate simple yet meaningful interaction among group members, with God's Word, and with the video teaching.

START
This section includes questions to get the conversation started, a review of the previous week's study to reinforce the content, and an introduction to the new content for the current week.

WATCH
This page includes key points from the video teaching, along with space for taking notes as participants watch the video.

DISCUSS
This page includes discussion questions that guide the group to respond to the video teaching and to relevant Bible passages.

PERSONAL STUDY

Two personal studies are provided each week to take individuals deeper into Scripture and to supplement the content introduced in the group study. With biblical teaching and interactive questions, these sections challenge individuals to grow in their understanding of God's Word and to make practical application to their lives.

LEADER GUIDE

On pages 166–173 at the back of this book, you'll find a leader guide that will help you prepare each week. Use this guide to gain a broad understanding of the content for each week and to learn ways you can engage with members at different levels of life-changing discussion.

AN OVERVIEW OF JAMES

The Book of James is a wonderful companion piece to Jesus' teachings as recorded in the four Gospels. James has a strong ethical emphasis that's consistent with the moral teachings Jesus gave to His disciples. James also mirrors the sometimes harsh rebukes Jesus spoke against religious hypocrisy. Like Jesus' teachings, the Book of James is a source of both exhortation and comfort, reproof and encouragement. While known for being extremely practical, James contains some of the most profound theological truths in the New Testament.

AUTHOR. James is named as the author in 1:1. A number of New Testament personalities were named James, but only three are candidates for the authorship of this book. James the son of Zebedee died in AD 44, too early to have been the author. No tradition names James the son of Alphaeus (Mark 3:18) as the author. This leaves James the brother of Jesus, also called James the Just (Mark 6:3; Acts 1:14; 12:17; 15:13; 21:18; 1 Cor. 15:7; Gal. 2:9,12), as the most likely candidate.

Scripture identifies James as the brother of Jesus in Matthew 13:55; Mark 6:3; and Galatians 1:19. Though he wasn't a follower of Christ during His earthly ministry (John 7:3-5), a post-resurrection appearance convinced James that Jesus is indeed the Christ (Acts 1:14; 1 Cor. 15:7). James later led the Jerusalem church (Gal. 2:9,12), exercising great influence there (Acts 1:14; 12:17; 15:13; 21:18; 1 Cor. 15:7; Gal. 2:9,12).

BACKGROUND. James was probably written between AD 48 and 52, though nothing in the epistle suggests a more precise date. James' death in AD 62 or 66 means the epistle was written before this time. Similarities to Gospel traditions and Pauline themes are suggestive. If Mark was written around AD 65 and time is allowed for the events of Acts 15 and 21 to have occurred between Paul's first and second missionary journeys, then a date between AD 48 and 52 seems most likely.

James led the Jerusalem church. The reference to “the twelve tribes in the Dispersion” (Jas. 1:1) suggests the letter was written to Jewish Christians living outside Israel. The reference to a synagogue in 2:2 also suggests that his audience was Jewish Christians. References to their circumstances (for example, oppression by wealthy landowners, 5:1-6) could refer to congregations anywhere in the Roman Empire.

MESSAGE AND PURPOSE. As a general epistle, James was addressed to a broad audience (Jewish Christians) rather than a specific audience (for example, Christians at Ephesus only). There’s an obvious concern to address internal and external difficulties that Jewish Christian congregations faced. Externally, they were facing trials (1:2), particularly oppression from wealthy landowners. It doesn’t appear that the oppression was religious in nature. Internally, it appears that dissension was caused by a lack of self-control (1:13-17), uncontrolled speech, and false teachings that led to a misunderstanding of true religion (1:19-27; 2:1-4; 3:1-8), favoritism toward the wealthy (2:1-13), and selfish ambition that opened the door to murder and criticism (4:1-12).

James addressed these issues primarily through the application of principles defined by the Old Testament wisdom tradition. The solutions he named reflected the wisdom from above that comes from “the Father of lights” (1:17), who generously gives wisdom to those who ask for it. Wisdom is required for proper speech in worship and for determining who ought to teach (1:19-27; 3:1-8). Wisdom is also needed to avoid internal conflicts that create dissension within congregations (3:13-18; 4:1-12). The theme of faith in action is also important (1:19-27; 2:14-26); James demonstrated that faith that doesn’t express itself in good works is useless. Another theme of the epistle is ethics, especially social justice (2:1-13; 4:1-12; 5:1-12).

STRUCTURE. The Book of James is a letter (an epistle), though only the greeting conforms to the ancient Greek form exemplified in Paul’s letters, especially Galatians.

The Book of James has also been compared to Old Testament wisdom literature. Although James contains wisdom elements, such as comparing the wisdom of the world with the wisdom that comes from God, it also contains exhortations and prophetic elements that aren’t common to wisdom literature.

WEEK 1

BROTHER/SERVANT

GROUP STUDY

START

Welcome everyone to Week 1 of James: Faith/Works.

Ask participants to introduce themselves with quick answers to the following question.

What's one phrase, nickname, or fact that summarizes who you are?

Today we begin a study of the Book of James. We'll start by simply looking at one verse—the introduction to the letter. Because all Scripture is the inspired Word of God, we can learn a lot from a greeting. James' introduction identifies the theme and tone of the entire letter.

Have you ever studied a book of the Bible? If so, what was it? How did you see the book differently after you completed your study?

James is a highly practical letter to Christians in the early church, but it's rooted in deep faith and rich theology. Maybe more than any other book in the New Testament, James emphasizes the application of Christian belief.

To prepare for the Week 1 video, pray that God will help each person understand and apply this truth:

James had a unique earthly relationship with Jesus, but his letter clarifies what the Christian life should look like for all believers. The Book of James is filled with practical wisdom, calling us to live out genuine faith through good works.

WATCH

Use the space below to take notes while you watch the Session 1 video.

1. You need to ______________________ what the Bible is saying about God's interest in you.

2. The sovereign King of Glory is not a __________. He is a __________.

3. God leads us into the ______________ possible life by revealing to us who He is.

4. It is ________ and ______ alone that will satisfy the longings of our heart.

5. God is so about God that the Bible itself, first and foremost, is about ________. It's not about ______.

6. God makes known to us the _________ _____ ________.

7. When God says, "Thou shalt not," He's not trying to ______ you of anything.

8. ___________________ and _________________ are the two ways God draws us into the fullest life possible.

9. God does not promise that we will ______ suffer, but rather that He will be with us in our suffering, and He will ____________ it.

10. Trials, suffering, and difficulty can be expected. They do not _______________ the heart of God.

11. This is about _____________ not _________________.

12. __________ and ________________ will not satisfy the soul.

ANSWERS: 1) personalize; 2) taker, giver; 3) fullest; 4) God, God; 5) God, you; 6) path of life; 7) rob; 8) Salvation, obedience; 9) not, redeem; 10) surprise; 11) progress, perfection; 12) Riches, comfort

DISCUSS

Use the following questions to guide your discussion of the video.

Three things to pay special attention to in the Book of James:

1. The Book of James was written to Jews who were dispersed from Jerusalem because of persecution. We can also expect to suffer for our faith, but God has promised to be with us.
2. The Book of James reveals that the Christian life is about progress, not perfection.
3. The Book of James reminds us again and again that the things of the world will never satisfy.

How did James describe himself as he opened his letter in James 1:1?

James, a servant of God and of the Lord Jesus Christ,
To the twelve tribes in the Dispersion: Greetings.
JAMES 1:1

Why is it significant that James, as a Jew, mentioned both God and Jesus?

What does the word *servant* mean in this verse? What does it tell us about James that he referred to himself this way? What does it suggest about the content of his letter? About his perspective on the Christian life?

The thief comes only to steal and kill and destroy. I came that they may have life and have it abundantly.
JOHN 10:10

How is the abundant life Jesus promise in John 10:10 related to the idea of Christians obeying Him as Lord?

Do you think of God as being more concerned with either your obedience or your joy? How does your perspective on God affect your daily life?

Your eyes saw my unformed substance;
in your book were written, every one of them,
the days that were formed for me,
when as yet there was none of them.
PSALM 139:16

How does believing that God created you and knows everything about you affect your willingness to obey Him?

Matt highlighted three major themes that will run throughout our study of James:

1. Trials, suffering, and difficulty can be expected. They never surprise God.
2. God desires progress, not perfection, as we follow Jesus.
3. Riches and comfort will never satisfy the soul.

As Matt highlighted the themes found in the Book of James, which ones stood out most to you? Why?

Which of these common struggles in the Christian life most often threatens to steal, kill, and destroy your joy and satisfaction?

On a scale of 1 to 10, with 1 being spiritually dead and 10 being fully alive in joyful obedience, how would you rate your relationship with Jesus? Explain your rating.

Progress, not perfection, is James' message on faith and works. Sanctification—being shaped in the likeness of Jesus—is an ongoing work of the Holy Spirit in your life. You hear the Holy Spirit's voice as you read the pages of Scripture.

Our goal is to move closer to being fully alive in Christ by the end of our thirteen-session journey through the Book of James.

What are your hopes and expectations for studying the Book of James?

What remaining questions or comments do you have about this session's video teaching or discussion?

What was challenging, convicting, encouraging, or timely for your current circumstances?

Close in prayer.

PRAYER REQUESTS

PERSONAL STUDY

PART 1: BROTHER

If you could gather all of the people who have ever lived—every person in history—James would stand out from the crowd as a man with a unique relationship to Jesus. The author of the biblical book bearing his name was also Jesus' little brother.

Technically, James and Jesus were half brothers. They shared an earthly mother, Mary, but James' biological father was Joseph, while Jesus was born of the Holy Spirit. He was the only begotten Son of God. Joseph was Jesus' earthly father, but he and Jesus weren't biologically related. However, James and Jesus were biologically related.

How's that for sibling rivalry? It's not tough to imagine the mixed feelings James probably experienced growing up with the world's greatest brother—literally. Jesus was God's gift to humanity.

As Jesus' ministry began to grow, opinions about Him also grew increasingly divided among the public and even in His own family.

Read Mark 3:13-19. List the names of Jesus' twelve disciples.

Maybe you never thought too much about it, but Jesus' own family members were noticeably absent. Look at their reaction in the next verses.

Read Mark 3:20-21. What did Jesus' family think about Jesus and why?

A few chapters later Jesus told the disciples He chose these words:

A prophet is not without honor, except in his hometown and among his relatives and in his own household.
MARK 6:4

Read Mark 6:1-4. Why was it difficult for people who knew Jesus to believe in Him?

Have you found spiritual conversations to be easier or more difficult among nonbelieving family and friends? Why?

Jesus' own family, including James, thought He was getting carried away with the whole religious thing. Put yourself in their shoes, and their reaction seems pretty reasonable. In Mark 3, Jesus' small-group discussion had gone so long and drawn so many people that He wasn't even able to eat. His family thought He was crazy!

Picture the scene. James and his family showed up to talk some sense into His oldest brother, but the house was so packed that they couldn't even get in to see Him. Frustrated and desperate, they had to ask someone to ask someone to ask Jesus to come out. On top of that, religious leaders among the crowd were accusing Jesus of being demon-possessed (Mark 3:22).

Read Mark 3:31-35. Why would Jesus' words have been shocking in that moment?

What changed about James' relationship with Jesus after he believed in Him? What's the difference between knowing about Jesus and truly knowing Him?

When have you heard or spoken a difficult truth that encouraged salvation or spiritual growth?

We're also still likely to do the same thing Jesus' family did. Especially in our comfortable American Christianity, it's easy to discourage people from being too devoted. Maybe you've had an ongoing conversation in your mind about how seriously you should take the whole Jesus thing. What if your faith meant a change in attitude, lifestyle, or spending? What if it meant sacrifice or difficulty? What if it meant doing something that made the rest of the world, even the people closest to you, think you'd lost your mind?

James was literally related to Jesus, but Jesus said that wasn't enough. The right family can't save you. People often say things like "I've always been a Christian," or assume they are because they were born into a family that occasionally went to church, celebrated Christmas, and maybe even observed Easter. But remember Jesus' words to his own mother and brothers.

Jesus was abundantly clear. Your family can't save you. A relationship with God is a matter of personal faith expressed through active obedience to the will of God.

Conclude this part of this week's personal study by praying about the following.

- ☐ **Have I been relying on my upbringing, my family, or my own reasoning to shape my view of God?**
- ☐ **Does total faith in Jesus seem unreasonable? Are certain areas of my life currently off limits to God?**
- ☐ **Am I seeking to know and do the will of God?**
- ☐ **How will I respond to Jesus today?**

Ask God to reveal Himself to you as you continue studying His Word so that you can know and do what pleases Him.

PART 2: SERVANT

Truly, truly, I say to you, unless one is born again he cannot see the kingdom of God.
JOHN 3:3

This was a radical statement among the Jews—God's chosen people. Jesus told a religious leader the same thing He told His own mother, Mary, and His own brothers, including James. Biology isn't enough. Tradition isn't enough.

Read John 3:1-21. In your own words, summarize Jesus' teaching on belief.

We can never be good enough. We need the cross. We need the resurrection. We need Jesus. We're saved by faith alone, by grace alone, through Christ alone.

When Jesus explained our need to be born again, He concluded by saying saving faith must be lived out in active obedience to the will of God our Father. This idea sounds familiar.

How did Jesus say our acts of obedience relate to our faith?

The people of God are born again into the Heavenly Father's family. We need a change of heart in order to experience abundant, eternal life with the King.

Read Ephesians 2:1-10 to see how the gospel becomes effective in our lives.

Everyone is or was once obedient to:

Why is this an important truth for believers?

You're saved by:

You're made for:

Why are these important truths for believers?

You haven't been saved by your good works, but it's absolutely clear throughout Scripture that you've been made for good works. Men and women who've been born again confidently walk in the light of Christ, doing the good works God has created them to do.

Faith works. Faith is sufficient for salvation. Faith is seen in good works. God does the saving. You do the serving.

The Book of James begins with the author identifying himself by name and as "a servant of God and of the Lord Jesus Christ" (Jas. 1:1). He was defined by his relationship of active faith and obedient service.

On a scale of 1 to 10, how likely would someone be to identify you as a servant of Jesus?

1 2 3 4 5 6 7 8 9 10
Would never cross their mind The most obvious thing about me

How would you explain the difference between calling yourself a Christian and being a servant of Jesus Christ?

We can easily miss what's going on here in our English translations. The original Greek text of the New Testament uses James' Hebrew name: Jacob. Not only would the original audience know James, the brother of Jesus and the leader in the Jerusalem church, but they would also catch the author's symbolic identification with his audience.

In biblical history Jacob was the father of the Jewish nation. After he wrestled with God, God renamed him Israel. Jacob had twelve sons who became the twelve tribes of Israel (Gen. 32:28; 35:9-11,22-26).

Later in biblical history, the Assyrians conquered the Northern Kingdom of Israel, and the Babylonians then conquered the Southern Kingdom. This period of captivity and oppression came to be referred to as the *dispersion*—the same word James used to address the early church audience: "to the twelve tribes in the Dispersion" (Jas. 1:1).

This simple form of address has profound significance. After Jesus' ascension, the Christian church was almost immediately persecuted and scattered from Jerusalem into Judea and Samaria, spreading the gospel to the Gentiles (Acts 1:8; 8:1).

Just as Jesus taught that the family of God is those who do the will of the Father, James presented the church as the faithful—the holy people of God's new covenant. In Acts 15:13-18, James publicly declared that the Old Testament prophecy of God's gathering His remnant was being fulfilled in the church.

James encouraged Christians to faithfully serve Jesus as their King. This encouragement would have been comforting and countercultural. When Jesus is Lord, we pledge our allegiance entirely to Him. This stance will put us at odds with our culture at some point.

In what ways does living for Jesus put Christians at odds with culture?

The Christian life isn't easy. Serving God through faithful obedience to Jesus won't equal health, wealth, and happiness in the earthly sense. In fact, Jesus promised that when we truly identify ourselves with Him, we'll experience persecution (John 15:20). James knew it. The early church knew it. It's still true today.

Prayerfully reflect on this question: *Am I willing to identify with Jesus and live for Him, no matter what?*

[Jesus] said to all, "If anyone would come after me, let him deny himself and take up his cross daily and follow me."
LUKE 9:23

WEEK 2

TRIALS / TEMPTATIONS

GROUP STUDY

START

Welcome everyone to the group. Take a minute to review Week 1 before starting Week 2.

Before starting the new content each week, we'll take a few minutes to review the personal study from the previous week. The review questions will focus on two general themes: faith—what we're learning in God's Word—and works—what we're doing as servants of Jesus.

FAITH. In what ways is your faith growing? What's one thing you learned through group discussion or personal study this past week?

WORKS. When did the message of James seem especially relevant this past week? How did you apply what you're learning to your daily life?

Reviewing the previous week's study serves two essential purposes.

1. Review sets the context for what we're about to study and discuss in Scripture.
2. Review provides accountability for putting into practice the things we're learning about God and about ourselves.

Remember, James focused on teaching the church that genuine faith in Jesus will result in living for Jesus. Faith works. We want to believe the truth in God's Word and put it into action in our lives. This week we begin examining the first major theme that runs throughout the Book of James.

To prepare for the Week 2 video, pray that God will help each person understand and apply this truth:

As believers, we'll face trials and temptations that test our faith and dependence on God. But enduring adversity ultimately brings joy.

WATCH

Use the space below to take notes while you watch the Session 2 video.

1. Trials will come, but count it all joy because God is ___________.
2. The ____________ meets us in the world that we are in.
3. Trials are a pathway to __________________.
4. Trials help me be ______________________ aware of my need for God.
5. You shouldn't feel ___________ or ___________ about wrestling with doubt.
6. God honors the __________.
7. The first fight is _____________. The second fight is ____________________.
8. It's all ___________ in the end.
9. We need to understand that _____________ make us consciously aware that we need ________.
10. God knew what He was _____________ on the cross.
11. He ___________ you.

ANSWERS: 1) good; 2) Bible; 3) maturity; 4) consciously; 5) guilt, shame; 6) fight; 7) doubt, comparison; 8) level; 9) trials, God; 10) buying; 11) chose

DISCUSS

Use the following questions to guide your discussion of the video.

Trials will come, but count it all joy because God is good.

How do we view trials as believers in Christ?

1. Trials are a pathway to maturity.
2. Trials help me be consciously aware of my need for God.

Two prayers in this text.

1. Grant me wisdom.
2. Increase my faith. Kill my doubts.

One of the greatest anchors for your soul when trials come, regardless of the intensity of those trials, is the greater your knowledge of the goodness and grace of God on your life the more likely you are to praise Him in the storm. God chose you. It was of His own will that He called you to Himself.

James started with the tough realities of life and rock-solid truths of God's character. He laid a foundational truth for us to rest on as Christians: God is good.

Why is it vital to have a right understanding of God's character?

Although it may sound overly simple to state that God is good, why is this specific quality a necessary truth to embrace?

Read James 1:5,12-13.

Every good gift and every perfect gift is from above, coming down from the Father of lights, with whom there is no variation or shadow due to change. Of his own will he brought us forth by the word of truth, that we should be a kind of firstfruits of his creatures.
JAMES 1:17-18

What does each verse reveal about God's goodness?

The video included the following point.

> *One of the greatest anchors for your soul in the trials that come, regardless of the intensity of those trials, is the knowledge of the goodness and grace of God in your life. The greater the knowledge of God's goodness and grace, especially in the world of common grace, the more likely you are to praise Him in the storm.*

What is meant by the term *common grace?* How does it differ from God's specific blessings in the lives of believers?

What examples do you see of common grace in your life?

How does common grace serve as an anchor in trials and storms?

The difference between a trial and a temptation is huge. Trials lead to God's glorification. Temptations look for self-gratification. Trials build strength. Temptations seek weakness. Trials require perseverance. Temptations offer shortcuts. You'll be tempted to doubt God's goodness when you experience various trials.

What promises or benefits result from trials?

How do trials provide a pathway to Christian maturity?

How do trials make you aware of your need for God?

Matt addressed two major struggles in relation to trials: doubt and comparison.

How would you describe the struggle of doubt? The struggle of comparison?

How does each of these struggles rob us of joy?

Which is a bigger struggle for you—doubt or comparison?

How does the fact that God chose us and is for us change our perspective on hardship?

What remaining questions or comments do you have about the video teaching or discussion?

What was challenging, convicting, encouraging, or timely for your current circumstances?

Close in prayer.

PRAYER REQUESTS

PERSONAL STUDY

PART 1: TRIALS

One thing you need to understand in order to feel the weight of what you're about to study is the fact that the Book of James (AD 48–52) was the first book written in what's now the New Testament. Nearly five hundred years passed after Malachi wrote the final words of Old Testament Scripture.

You don't just pick up parchment and decide to write a letter to God's people. This wasn't the age of blogs, social media, or talking heads on news networks. What would prompt somebody to address people he had never met?

The Spirit of God had an urgent yet eternal word for the church in that moment as well as for us today. So the first details we need to know are who James' audience was and why God spoke to them.

James, the half brother of Jesus, wrote this letter to believers outside Palestine. This was a decade, maybe less, after the death, burial, resurrection, and ascension of Christ.

Let's put this time frame in context. If we're tracking the early church's progress as recorded in the Book of Acts, we're not even halfway through the book yet. In fact, believers were just starting to be called *Christians* (Acts 11:26), which was originally an offensive term used to mock followers of Jesus. Christians had scattered, but Paul hadn't been sent on his first missionary journey yet.

Read Acts 12:1-5 and summarize what happened to James the apostle (not the author of this letter) and to Peter.

How did the church respond to this persecution? What can its example teach you about trials?

The historical events recorded in Acts 12, including the martyrdom of one of Jesus' twelve apostles and Peter's second angelic deliverance from prison, set the stage for James' letter.

Read James 1:2-3, likely the first sentence in the Bible ever written to Christians.

Count it all joy, my brothers, when you meet trials of various kinds, for you know that the testing of your faith produces steadfastness.
JAMES 1:2-3

Underline the term James used to address Christians. How does this phrase parallel Jesus' teaching and make a bold statement about the nature of the Christian life?

Draw a circle around the word *joy*.

Draw a square around the word *trials*.

Peter was literally facing a trial of the legal kind. Many Christians were literally facing life-or-death situations. Persecution is still a reality for Christians throughout the world today, but these aren't the only kinds of trials worthy of mention in Scripture or worthy of the Spirit's comfort through the Word of God. James said trials of *various* kinds. Family, health, school, and relationships can all be trials.

In the left column, identify past or present trials in your life. In the right column, record anything good that came from the experiences or record a specific characteristic of God's goodness that helped you endure the trials.

Trial	Joy

Peter and James, two key leaders in the early church in Jerusalem, were experts on trials and suffering. They witnessed firsthand the hostility toward Jesus, and they led the earliest church through persecution.

Read what Peter wrote to his fellow Christians in 1 Peter 4:12-19.

There's a dangerously deceptive idea floating around that's often referred to as the prosperity gospel. It's a false gospel. It's not the gospel at all. It's heresy. The Bible doesn't teach that if we believe or give enough, God will make us healthy, wealthy, and successful in everything we do. On the contrary, the Bible often talks about trials as a pathway to maturity, leading us to greater dependence on God.

Yes, God is for us—always. Yes, God is good—always. Yes, God blesses His children—always. But that doesn't always mean we'll have health, wealth, and comfort. Sometimes it means we'll go through the fire, purifying and strengthening our faith.

Peter said not to be surprised when we face trials. Peter wasn't referring to trials that come just because we live in a fallen world broken by sin. He was specifically referring to trials that come as the direct result of being a Christian and living out your faith. It will happen. Guaranteed.

The good news is that vindication and victory are also guaranteed. Jesus Christ, who suffered unjustly to the point of death, was not only resurrected but is also coming back to judge the righteous and the unrighteous. Fiery trials will shed light on the truth: Jesus is Lord. He's worthy. He's good. Our suffering is never pointless:

Blessed is the man who remains steadfast under trial, for when he has stood the test he will receive the crown of life, which God has promised to those who love him.
JAMES 1:12

Thank God for His goodness, asking for joy and perseverance in the midst of various trials, especially those that come as a result of boldly living out your Christian faith.

PART 2: TEMPTATIONS

Scripture doesn't shy away from the realities of trials and temptations. An entire book in the Bible is dedicated to the trials and temptations of one man—Job. Many scholars believe the Book of Job is the oldest book in the Bible.

Job's story is an offshoot. His life isn't a link in the chain connecting God's creative work through Adam to His saving work through Jesus. No genealogy or geography surrounds Job's family to provide a context for his situation. He was simply a man with a personal relationship with the Lord—a man of deep faith.

Read Job 1:1–2:10 and list what this passage reveals about the awareness and ability of each figure.

God:

Satan:

Job:

Why is it important to recognize that God and Satan aren't equal opponents?

Why is it significant that the Bible includes the story of Job?

What does this story reveal about trials and temptations?

God's goodness is foundational to faith in the Christian life. His goodness is the hope we cling to. It's an anchor of truth when we're tossed by the raging seas of doubt. God is good to us, even in our trials.

Temptation, when boiled down to its most basic form, is doubting that God is good. It's the suspicion that something might be better than what He offers us. At the heart of sin is a denial that God is good or at least that He's good enough. Every man and woman ever to draw a breath has fallen for the same lie the serpent whispered in the garden: *God is keeping something good from you. Choose for yourself what's good* (Gen. 3:1-10).

Read James 1:12-18.

What two things does God never do?

1.

2.

What two things come only from God?

1.

2.

How can knowing these four things help you resist temptation?

It's important to distinguish between temptation and sin. Being tempted by something is not the same thing as sinning. That may sound obvious, but a lot of people carry an oppressive burden of guilt about temptations they face. Even if they never give in to temptation, committing sin, they struggle through life feeling defeated and joyless simply because they're tempted.

Job experienced difficult trials and was tempted to deny God's goodness, but he didn't sin. Generations later Jesus was tempted by Satan, but He didn't sin. Ever.

Read Hebrews 2:18 and 4:15. Summarize what they say about Jesus and temptation.

God isn't looking down from heaven shaking His head and wagging His finger in disgust and disapproval of our temptation. Jesus was tempted. In *every* way. So temptation itself isn't wrong. Don't beat yourself up. But don't give in or dismiss it as no big deal either. Jesus resisted. And by His Spirit you can too.

No temptation has overtaken you that is not common to man. God is faithful, and he will not let you be tempted beyond your ability, but with the temptation he will also provide the way of escape, that you may be able to endure it.
1 CORINTHIANS 10:13

What does this verse reveal about God and His relationship with you?

Identify areas of temptation in your life and truths that will remind you of ways to escape those temptations.

Temptations (Enticements)	Truth (Escape)

Pray for wisdom in how to live faithfully (Jas. 1:5). God promises to answer that prayer—always.

WEEK 3

HEARER

DOER

GROUP STUDY

START

Welcome everyone to the group. Take a minute to review Week 2 before starting Week 3.

Before starting new content, we'll take a few minutes to review the previous week, keeping in mind that the Christian life is one of transformation, not just information. The overarching message of James is that our faith expresses itself in our works.

FAITH. In what ways is your faith growing? What's one thing you learned through group discussion or personal study this past week?

WORKS. When did the message of James seem especially relevant this past week? How did you apply what you're learning to your daily life?

We've now laid a foundation for the Book of James and addressed the fact that life is difficult—even for Christians. In life, especially when facing trials and temptations, we'll constantly face the same decision: Will we do what God's Word says? That question will present itself in different circumstances, but underneath the surface the main point is the same.

This week Beau Hughes will fill in for Matt Chandler to finish James 1 with a great message on hearing and doing what God says.

To prepare for the Week 3 video, pray that God will help each person understand and apply this truth:

True belief causes Christians to live out their faith according to God's Word. We don't passively hear the Word. Rather, action should always follow genuine heart change.

WATCH

Use the space below to take notes while you watch the Week 3 video.

1. God's not the one that's ________________ you to sin.

2. God, out of His own goodness, love, and grace, brought us forth and caused us to be __________ __________.

3. God has decided to ______________ and _______________ all things to Himself.

4. What actually transforms character is ______________.

5. ___________ don't transform.

6. Take off all manner of ______________________ and ________________ and receive, put on, welcome, absorb, submit yourself to meekly humble yourself and receive the Word of God.

7. __________________ faith in the gospel is what pleases God.

8. This is the message of ____________: Left to ourselves, we can't and don't please God. But God has made a way for us to bring Him pleasure and to be accepted by God and that's through what ___________ ____________ has done.

9. Meekly receiving the Word of truth means more than just hearing it and nodding to it; it means to ________________ it and to actually, in faith, _______ upon it.

10. That word ____________ doesn't just mean to not remember; it also means you _________________.

ANSWERS: 1) tempting; 2) born again; 3) redeem, reconcile; 4) beauty; 5) Rules; 6) filthiness, wickedness; 7) Humble; 8) Christianity, Jesus Christ; 9) embrace; act 10) "faith"; discard

DISCUSS

Use the following questions to guide your discussion of the video.

Many scholars have called the Book of James a commentary on Jesus' Sermon on the Mount. They mean James uses similar language and images to describe a life of true faith. The Sermon on the Mount concluded with a famous parable about building a house.

Can someone summarize the parable comparing the two men who built one house on the sand and one house on the rock (Matt. 7:24-27)?

What did the two men have in common? What distinguished the two men from each other?

What was Jesus' point in this parable? How did He describe our only two options in life?

This is the heart of James' letter: hearing and doing, faith expressed in our works.

How did James' earthly relationship with Jesus lend credibility and passion to his message of being a doer, not just a hearer, of truth?

But be doers of the word, and not hearers only, deceiving yourselves. For if anyone is a hearer of the word and not a doer, he is like a man who looks intently at his natural face in a mirror. For he looks at himself and goes away and at once forgets what he was like. But the one who looks into the perfect law, the law of liberty, and perseveres, being no hearer who forgets but a doer who acts, he will be blessed in his doing.

JAMES 1:22-25

What was James trying to communicate with his mirror illustration?

In the video Beau said, “Rules don’t transform, only beauty transforms.”

What did he mean? How does this statement help us think about religion and our relationship with God?

Why do we need both motivation and rules?

Why isn’t “the law of liberty” (v. 25) a contradictory term? What’s “the perfect law” (v. 25)? How does it give freedom?

In Week 2 we discussed ways a right understanding of God’s character shapes our lives. This week we’ll see how a right understanding of our identities also affects our lives.

What did James mean when he said we deceive ourselves (v. 22)?

James identified our language, relationships, and attitudes as visible reflections of what’s in our hearts. Today’s video focused primarily on controlling our tongues.

If anyone thinks he is religious and does not bridle his tongue but
deceives his heart, this person’s religion is worthless.
Religion that is pure and undefiled before God the Father is this:
to visit orphans and widows in their affliction,
and to keep oneself unstained from the world.
JAMES 1:26-27

How well does your speech reflect the truth of who you are in Christ?

When are you most likely to lose control of your tongue?

What does losing control of our tongues suggest about where we're looking for our identity in that moment? How do we see ourselves in that moment?

What can we do this week to help one another live out the truth of the gospel—the perfect law of freedom? When and where do you need reminders of who God is and who you are in Christ?

What remaining questions or comments do you have about the video teaching or discussion?

What was challenging, convicting, encouraging, or timely for your current circumstances?

Close in prayer.

PRAYER REQUESTS

PERSONAL STUDY

PART 1: HEARER

He who has ears, let him hear.
MATTHEW 13:9

When Jesus taught with parables, He often concluded with a phrase like this. He called for people to hear and sometimes to see the truth if they were able. Jesus wasn't referring to physical senses but to spiritual discernment.

This particular statement comes after the parable of the sower, or the parable of the seed and the soil. In Jesus' story a sower casts seed on four types of soil and has four different results.

Read Matthew 13:1-9 and fill in the first two columns of the chart. Then read verses 18-23 to complete the final column.

Soil Type	Result	Spiritual Meaning

When studying the Bible, it's important not only to understand what God's Word says but also to consider your heart and how you're hearing truth. In other words, is the truth being received, taking root, and bearing fruit in your life?

On a scale of 1 to 10, how would you rate the current condition of your heart?

1 2 3 4 5 6 7 8 9 10

Lifeless **Fertile**

Have you received the gospel of salvation as true? If so, when did it first take root in your life?

Would you use the word *joy* to describe your response to the gospel? What other words would you use?

What social pressure do you face or fear for your Christian beliefs?

What causes stress in your life?

How do stress and daily busyness discourage your spiritual growth?

Do the ambitions in your life compete with or complement your faith? Explain.

In what areas are you experiencing spiritual growth and new life?

Hearing the truth—truly receiving it in such a way that it takes root and produces spiritual life—will transform your life. The growth rate isn't the same for everyone, but true believers in Jesus will produce fruit.

Read James 1:19-21. Notice that Jesus' teaching echoes in James' words, especially the phrase "implanted word" (v. 21).

What effect does being "quick to hear" (v. 19) have on your relationship with God?

Why should you be quick to hear in your relationships with other people?

One fruit of our new lives in Christ is a desire for truth and righteousness. God's truth and His righteousness are life-giving. In the midst of trials, temptations, and the pressures of life, our opinions, arguments, and self-righteous efforts will never accomplish godly change. Not for ourselves. Not for anyone.

Think about the phrase "be quick" (v. 19). Is hearing God a priority in your life? Identify the amount of time you spend listening to God.

	Time per Day	Total Time per Week
Prayer		
God's Word		
Christian community		
Corporate worship		
Other		

If you don't have a usual routine for prioritizing time in prayer and Scripture, this is the perfect time to start. In addition to the Book of James, the stanzas of Psalm 119 are a great starting point for nurturing a heart that desires to know God.

Try it now. Turn the words of Psalm 119:1-40 into a personal prayer.

PART 2: DOER

Hearing in a way that matters—in which God's truth is implanted in your heart, taking root and bearing fruit—will result in righteous activity. What you believe directs the way you live.

Read James 1:22. What's happening in your heart if you hear the Word but don't do what it says?

Give an example of a clear command of Scripture you've heard but haven't always obeyed.

Why is doing what you know to do often much more difficult than knowing what to do?

Read Romans 2:13. How does this verse complement James 1:22?

The Christian life is one of active obedience. When you hear God's Word, respond in obedience. All of the Bible study in the world is meaningless if it doesn't transform your affections and your actions.

In fact, knowledge can begin to harden your heart if your perspective is primarily focused inward. If your spiritual life is all input with no outlet, you start to spoil, like the roots to a potted plant without a drain. The right amount of water is life-giving to a potted plant. Too much water will begin to poison the same plant. There has to be a healthy balance between what's poured into the plant and its ability to absorb what it receives for healthy growth and ultimately for replication—flowers, fruit, seeds, or new shoots.

Look at another warning Paul gave to Christians who were growing arrogant and self-centered in their so-called spiritual maturity.

"Knowledge" puffs up, but love builds up.
1 CORINTHIANS 8:1

In Week 1 you saw that James was Jesus' half brother, yet he identified with Christ as Lord. During Jesus' ministry, when His family went to take Him out of a crowded teaching session, Jesus replied with words that must have sunk deep into James' heart:

My mother and my brothers are those
who hear the word of God and do it.
LUKE 8:21

James left no room in his letter for the idea of hearing the truth and not doing what it says. He didn't want his readers to deceive themselves into thinking they could be Christians merely by believing the right things about Jesus. Following Jesus requires action. As a disciple, you not only have to believe Christ is worth following, but you also have to take steps of faith to deny yourself, pick up your cross, and follow Him daily (Luke 9:23).

Read James 1:19-27, paying attention to what James said about hearing and doing.

Being a doer has two components: putting away filthiness and seeking pure religion. If the word *religion* gets you bent out of shape, set aside your personal interpretation of what that means. James was talking about a devoted life that's pleasing to God.

PUTTING AWAY FILTHINESS. The phrase used in verse 21, "Put away all filthiness," calls to mind an image like dirty laundry. Everyone has proverbial dirty laundry or dirty little secrets, which are just other ways of referring to sin. James later instructed the church to keep themselves "unstained from the world" (v. 27). What James called "rampant wickedness" (v. 21) includes obvious filthiness and stains Christians easily recognize as sinful and must turn away from.

Identify sins in each category in your life.

Rampant wickedness: **What obvious sins were part of your life before you repented and followed Christ as Savior and Lord?**

***All filthiness:* What dirty laundry do you need to take off? What sins do you still struggle with as a Christian?**

***Unstained from the world:* What attitudes and ambitions of your culture tempt you?**

If you have a difficult time identifying impure, selfish desires, ask yourself: *When, where, and about what do I get angry? When, where, and about what am I most likely to say something I shouldn't?*

SEEKING PURE RELIGION. Throughout generations and cultures, people have asked the question: What should a relationship with God look like? James' answer is shocking because it doesn't focus on behaviors to please God. Instead, he offered a simple description of controlling the tongue and caring for other people. A right relationship with God will be evident in right relationships with other people.

Jesus said people would know His disciples by their love for one another (John 13:35). Christlike love is most evident in relationships in which the other people have nothing to offer in return. This kind of love is countercultural. It's selfless. It's righteous.

Orphans and widows are vulnerable and have nothing to offer in return for kindness, especially in a first-century context in which Christians were a persecuted subculture. God expects us to go out of our way to love the overlooked, marginalized, vulnerable, and needy. Why? Because that's exactly what the Creator of the universe did for us (Rom. 5:8; Phil. 2:4-9).

Ask God to give you spiritual ears to hear His truth and eyes to see opportunities to put it into action. Also pray for a humble heart that's eager to respond to other people in Christlike love.

WEEK 4

JUDGMENT / MERCY

GROUP STUDY

START

Welcome everyone to the group. Take a minute to review Week 3 before starting Week 4.

Before starting new content, we'll take a few minutes to review the previous week, keeping in mind that the Christian life is one of transformation, not just information. The overarching message of James is that our faith expresses itself in our works.

FAITH. In what ways is your faith growing? What's one thing you learned through group discussion or personal study this past week?

WORKS. When did the message of James seem especially relevant this past week? How did you apply what you're learning to your daily life?

This week we'll begin the second chapter of James. The first chapter introduced several topics and themes. Now we'll begin focusing on specific situations. James concluded the first chapter by saying that we must be not only hearers of the Word but also doers. Otherwise, we settle for an impure, defiled religion that's focused on our own interests. Today's text stands in stark contrast to caring for widows and orphans; instead, the stain of worldliness was polluting the church with favoritism for the rich. Simply put, they weren't putting the teachings of Jesus into practice.

To prepare for the Week 4 video, pray that God will help each person understand and apply this truth:

We sin when we show partiality to some people over others, whether they're rich, poor, or different in any other way. Believers should extend mercy rather than harsh judgment to others.

WATCH

Use the space below to take notes while you watch the Session 4 video.

1. In this space, the name of Christ is being ______________, the witness of the church is __________, and the gladness of heart of those present is being sucked dry.

2. To be ____________ and _________________ and ______________ toward the needy and broken is to be made visible in your heart a failure to understand what the gospel message actually is.

3. ______________ do not save us. We are saved by grace alone, through faith alone,

4. Do not withhold or give glory, love, affection, hospitality, friendship, mercy, kindness, or service to people based upon their ____________________ ________________________.

5. You __________________ God and reveal you don't understand the gospel when you show __________________.

6. You were not saved because of your ________________________.

7. The incessant need that we have to be seen as __________ and ___________________ must die.

8. If you want to please the heart of God, _____ _______ ___________.

9. Faith without mercy toward others is not _________________ faith.

10. Genuine faith means there's ________________, not _________________.

11. In your remembrance of God's ______________ grace and mercy, ___________ it to others.

ANSWERS: 1) soiled, gone; 2) blind, unmoved, static; 3) Works; 4) external experience; 5) dishonor, partiality; 6) awesomeness; 7) cool, relevant; 8) do the Word; 9) genuine 10) progress, perfection; 11) forgiving, extend

DISCUSS

Use the following questions to guide your discussion of the video.

As King, Jesus has demands.

What's your immediate reaction to that statement? What comes to mind when you hear the word *King?* When you hear the word *demands?*

Honestly, do you typically think about Jesus as King? In what other ways do you think about Jesus? How does the way you view Jesus affect the way you relate to Him and His words?

Matt introduced today's teaching with this statement:

In the warning there's an invitation to something better.

What does that statement mean? How is this a life-changing perspective on God's authority and His commands in Scripture?

How does the image of God as Father help us understand "the perfect law, the law of liberty" we discussed last week in James 1:25?

What does the following statement mean?

Christians aren't perfect but should be making progress.

In what ways is this view of sanctification—the process of growing in holiness and Christlikeness—encouraging?

Matt continued that thought with a strong statement about the absence of progress in the Christian life:

Where there's no progress, there should be questions.

What does that statement mean?

How does this logical conclusion, based on the previous view of sanctification, challenge you?

Today's video applied this view of sanctification in the Christian life to our natural tendency to be partial. In other words, our flesh distorts judgment and mercy with self-serving motives.

Read James 2:1-13. As you read, jot down the what, why, and better way addressed in the video.

What:

Why:

Better Way:

What's a Christian supposed to do or not do, according to this passage?

Without sharing specific details, when have you been hurt by unfair judgment, partiality, or exclusiveness in the church?

Why should we obey the command not to judge or show partiality as individuals? As a church community?

What's the better way presented in these verses? How does the better way invite us into greater joy and satisfaction?

Whom can we as individuals or as a group reach out to include?

What remaining questions or comments do you have about the video teaching or discussion?

What was challenging, convicting, encouraging, or timely for your current circumstances?

Close in prayer.

PRAYER REQUESTS

PERSONAL STUDY

PART 1: JUDGMENT

The language of "family" is key in James' letter to the dispersed church. For followers of Jesus, true faith is personal, but it's also shared. The church is the family of God.

When addressing the nature of temptation, James referred to God as "the Father of lights" (Jas. 1:17). When describing "religion that is pure and undefiled," James again referred to God as Father (v. 27). Notice that the religion that pleases the Father is caring for widows and orphans—women and children without families. In these verses, James turned his attention to another marginalized group: the poor.

Almost every time James addressed a practical point of application, he used a key phrase to draw attention to what he was about to say, pleading in love with his fellow church members.

Read James 2:1. What term is used to identify Christians?

Summarize the foundational truth behind this term of identification.

How does the command in verse 1 naturally follow from the identification?

If the Christian life is a shared life, there's no room for favoritism, partiality, and discrimination. Christians are related by blood. Because we share the name of Christ by the blood of Jesus, we're brothers and sisters, born again into the family of God the Father through faith in His only Son. Your brothers and sisters are no more or less members of your family based on what they wear or what they own. Worldly relations are based on benefit. Family relationships are based on blood.

The church is a family. You don't get the benefit of a church family without loving the crazy uncle or the embarrassing sibling. No matter what they have to offer, how they look, or what they've done, family is family. It's antigospel, flying in the face of Jesus' sacrificial love and grace, to treat people as more or less worthy of a seat in our Father's house.

Read James 2:1-13.

What do you typically value in other people? If you're honest, how much of that is based on external factors like popularity, personal style, or attractiveness?

How are those standards different from the way James calls us to treat people in the church?

What types of people would you choose to avoid if they came to your church? How much would you say those judgments are based on external factors?

When have you benefited from a relationship with a brother or sister in Christ who's very different from you?

If you have no relationships with fellow Christians who are different from you, how can you change that?

The temptation of a selfish heart is to see other people in terms of what they have to offer. We dehumanize people, weighing their worth against how we think they will benefit us. Sometimes we're tempted to turn relationships into nothing more than an exchange of time and energy, where we hope to get as much out of it as we put into it. Will this person be able to add to my sense of self-worth and increase popularity? Will kindness to this person result in perks? What will I get from being a friend with this person?

Read James 1:9-11. What do these verses say about earthly wealth?

Why are these verses an important reminder for the way we view ourselves? For the way we view others?

Read 1 Peter 1:13-25. What phrases and themes in Peter's letter are similar to those in James' letter?

What two things did Peter identify as having transcendent value in verses 18-19,23-25?

Complete this sentence to summarize Peter's point in verses 13-25:

Because we value ________________, we'll ________________.

When we put a tag on someone's worth, for any reason, we ignore the fact that Christ paid the ultimate price for us all. Jesus willingly paid the same price for other people as He did for us. The same gospel that saved us is the same gospel that unites us with brothers and sisters in Christ. His blood bought our freedom from sin and made us sons and daughters of the Father of lights.

Pray for a humble heart that overflows with love for brothers and sisters in Christ—no matter what they have or don't have to offer in return.

PART 2: MERCY

The church family is a countercultural community. We live by different standards than the world does. We're called into a different story than the rest of the world, because we serve a different King and are citizens of a different kingdom.

Read 1 John 4:7-21. Pay attention to the connection between a person's relationship with God and with other people.

What connection exists between the sincerity of our faith in God and the way we treat other people?

This countercultural, counterintuitive, brotherly love is the pure and undefiled religion James summarized at the end of chapter 1. Though it necessarily includes them, our love isn't limited to widows and orphans. Christian love manifests itself in various ways. James moved straight into another scenario in chapter 2.

Reread James 1:27–2:13 to refresh your memory.

Do you see the relation between expressing true religion and refusing to show partiality? Visiting orphans and widows in their distress and not showing partiality to the rich over the poor are two sides of the same coin. Judging the worth of other people is a worldly stain on pure Christian religion. Preferring the rich over the poor, the influential over the ordinary, and people who can benefit us over widows and orphans defiles the church and the message of the gospel. Essentially, this mentality is idolatrous, making church about us and what we can get out of it rather than about God and what He has given to us in Jesus.

So while the world naturally associates with the rich and powerful and chases after fame and popularity, Christians intentionally go out of their way to honor people who've been pushed to the fringes of society.

Honestly, are there certain people you struggle to love? If so, who and why?

Whom would you find it difficult to honor in your church if they showed up and sat next to you? Why?

An honest search of your heart will reveal that you don't like some people. Sometimes those feelings may be reasonable. For example, someone may have treated you terribly. Other times your feelings are a snap judgment based purely on personality, appearance, or culture. People may talk, act, or dress a certain way that you find off-putting or difficult. Maybe you find them annoying, awkward, tactless, or not quite like you in some way. They're just different.

Scripture isn't saying you have to be best friends with everybody. But Christian community should be more than friendly. It should be family. We're brothers and sisters. We have to treat everyone with equal dignity and should be quick to extend the same love and mercy to others that Christ has shown to us.

James referred to the royal law from Scripture, "You shall love your neighbor as yourself" (2:8). Judaism interpreted this quotation from Leviticus 19:18 as a summation of a perfectly religious life. A true love for God and for other people was the essence of the entire Jewish law. Think again about two sides of a single coin. You can't have one without the other. They're inseparable.

Read Jesus' teaching on fulfilling this law in Luke 10:25-37.

What did the lawyer ask Jesus, and why did he ask (v. 29)?

Who proved to be a neighbor (vv. 36-37)? Why would this have been controversial to Jesus' original audience?

What can you conclude from the fact that Jesus answered the question "Who is my neighbor?" by asking, "Who proved to be a neighbor?"

Read another parable of Jesus in Matthew 18:21-35.

Summarize the point of this parable in your own words.

What did God put on your heart as you read this passage? How will you respond to what God revealed?

The parable of the good Samaritan illustrates a pure and undefiled heart that was revealed in mercy toward someone in need. The supposed religious characters in the story proved to have hearts stained by the world. True religion that pleases God the Father was seen in mercy.

The parable of the unforgiving servant revealed a heart stained by the world, indifferent to another person's need. Once again, the story reveals the gross nature of withholding mercy and judging others with a standard by which God hasn't judged us.

An honest assessment of your heart will reveal that it's still selfish and prideful in certain places. You probably have more prejudices than you realize. You probably have a greater sense of entitlement than you'd like to admit. You certainly have more pride than you're aware of. You may be slow or unwilling to forgive. The human heart is deeply broken. Acknowledging this fact and crying out to God for healing is the first step of healing. Once you recognize your own sinfulness and hopeless brokenness, you can be reconciled to God and begin showing merciful love to others.

Close your time in prayer, confessing and repenting of sinful attitudes in your heart. Ask for a humble, merciful heart, eager to be a neighbor to people around you. Let Jesus' words sink deep into your heart, taking root and bearing the fruit of true religion that pleases our Father:

Those who are well have no need of a physician, but those who are sick. Go and learn what this means: "I desire mercy, and not sacrifice." For I came not to call the righteous, but sinners.
MATTHEW 9:12-13

WEEK 5

FAITH / WORKS

GROUP STUDY

START

Welcome everyone to the group. Take a minute to review Week 4 before starting Week 5.

Before starting new content, we'll take a few minutes to review the previous week, keeping in mind that the Christian life is one of transformation, not just information. The overarching message of James is that our faith will be expressed in our works.

FAITH. In what ways is your faith growing? What's one thing you learned through group discussion or personal study this past week?

WORKS. When did the message of James seem especially relevant this past week? How did you apply what you're learning to your daily life?

Hopefully, you recognized opportunities to extend mercy and kindness this week.

James introduced the idea of hearing and doing at the end of chapter 1, along with a definition of pure and undefiled religion. Chapter 2 then put a spotlight on a specific example of worldly behavior in the church that contradicted that definition and the biblical standard of loving God and loving our neighbors. This week we'll consider his argument for why our actions and beliefs must line up with each other. This is the heart of James' message. Faith works.

To prepare for the Week 5 video, pray that God will help each person understand and apply this truth:

Faith and works are never found apart. In fact, James tells us faith apart from works is dead. Works don't save us, but good works should follow true faith.

WATCH

Use the space below to take notes while you watch the Session 5 video.

1. Weak as we are in the ____________, we cannot fulfill the ___________.

2. James is not arguing that works must be added to faith, but rather that ____________, _______________ faith will inevitably be characterized by works.

3. Faith without works is ________________.

4. You have been _______________ by God and are now to be a conduit, through which the ________________ of God flow.

5. Faith without works _________________ save us.

6. ________________________ assent to correct doctrine is not salvation.

7. The _______________ of the Bible is that faith alone saves you, but not faith that is _______________.

8. Faith without works is __________.

9. There is no __________.

10. It's ______________ that leads to _____________________ that determines ______________.

11. The works of the saint are to _______________ and ___________ the Lord.

ANSWERS: 1) flesh, law; 2) genuine, biblical; 3) useless; 4) blessed, blessings; 5) cannot; 6) Intellectual; 7) unity, alone; 8) dead; 9) list; 10) desire, discipline, destiny; 11) know, love

DISCUSS

Use the following questions to guide your discussion of the video.

What effect does it have to believe God delights in you—that He not only loves you in a broad sense of the word but also specifically and affectionately likes you?

Why is delighting in the Lord a vital part of faith and works?

How did James use the term *faith?* The term *works?*

How is keeping the law different from works that are characteristic of faith?

James didn't argue that we must add works to our faith. To add anything to our faith is to say the cross means nothing.

What does it mean for the cross to be sufficient?

In the video Matt discussed the main point in this portion of James' letter by examining these four ideas about faith without works:

- It is useless.
- It cannot save.
- It is ineffective.
- It is dead.

How would you explain the main point from the video teaching?

Let's consider ways this reality plays out personally in our lives.

What good is it, my brothers, if someone says he has faith but does not have works? Can that faith save him? If a brother or sister is poorly clothed and lacking in daily food, and one of you says to them, "Go in peace, be warmed and filled," without giving them the things needed for the body, what good is that? So also faith by itself, if it does not have works, is dead.

JAMES 2:14-17

What are some statements we say that sound Christian without thinking or without acting on them?

On a scale of 1 to 10, 1 meaning you never do anything and 10 meaning you always do something, how often do you actually pray for people when you say you will? How often do you try to help meet a need?

Read James 2:18-26.

Understanding this next point could literally save your soul. Especially if you've grown up in church, you might mistakenly think salvation is a matter of believing the right things about Jesus, like a code that unlocks the gates of heaven.

Read the following statement.

Belief in what the Bible says isn't salvation.

What does the statement mean? How does it challenge the way you view Christianity? How does it affect the way you share the gospel?

What's your reaction to James' statement that even demons believe in God (v. 19)?

What do you think it means for demons to shudder? How does this reality convict us about the nature of saving faith and works?

James pointed to the lives of Abraham and Rahab as examples of people who did more than just believe and shudder—they acted as the evidence of saving faith.

How do the examples of Abraham and Rahab, seemingly polar opposites in every earthly way, encourage you in your faith?

What remaining questions or comments do you have about the video teaching or discussion?

What was challenging, convicting, encouraging, or timely for your current circumstances?

Close in prayer.

PRAYER REQUESTS

PERSONAL STUDY

PART 1: FAITH

What's true faith? The word *faith* is thrown around a lot today. It can be used to refer to organized religion, positive thinking, generic hope, and self-confidence. So when we talk about faith and belief and being a believer in Jesus, it's important that we understand the biblical meaning of *faith*.

Start by writing out your own definition of *faith*.

Maybe the two clearest verses in Scripture for defining *faith* are found in the Book of Hebrews in a chapter that has become known as the hall of faith.

Read Hebrews 11:1. Summarize the importance of faith.

Read Hebrews 11:6. Summarize the importance of faith.

Hebrews 11 provides a summary of biblical history, highlighting the faith of key individuals along the way. If it sounds daunting to read an entire chapter outside of James right now, think of it as a blog post, a video review, or a highlight reel: "The Old Testament in Sixty Seconds." It's a quick read.

Take a moment to read Hebrews 11.

The Book of James has sometimes been misunderstood as contradicting the idea of salvation by faith alone, as taught in other parts of the New Testament like the writings of Paul and what you just read in Hebrews.

Though they may appear contradictory in their use of terms, Hebrews and James actually teach the same thing about the nature of true faith. Compare the following verses on the lives of Abraham and Rahab.

Circle the phrases "by faith" and "by works" in the following verses.

By faith Abraham, when he was tested, offered up Isaac, and he who had received the promises was in the act of offering up his only son.
HEBREWS 11:17

Was not Abraham our father justified by works when he offered up his son Isaac on the altar?
JAMES 2:21

By faith Rahab the prostitute did not perish with those who were disobedient, because she had given a friendly welcome to the spies.
HEBREWS 11:31

Was not also Rahab the prostitute justified by works when she received the messengers and sent them out by another way?
JAMES 2:25

Underline the action described in each verse.

A key to good Bible study is to consider context, especially when teachings appear contradictory. The author of Hebrews suggested that Abraham and Rahab are examples because of their faith, while James seemed to suggest they're examples because of their works. On closer inspection their essential point is the same.

You see that a person is justified by works and not by faith alone.
JAMES 2:24

James was clarifying that true faith expresses itself in works. If you really believe, you'll act on your faith. Paul and the writer of Hebrews would agree 100 percent with James on this point. Look at the following verses written by Paul, for example:

By grace you have been saved through faith.
And this is not your own doing; it is the gift of God,
not a result of works, so that no one may boast.
EPHESIANS 2:8-9

Paul's point wasn't that works are unrelated and irrelevant to our faith. His point was that we don't deserve or earn God's favor through good behavior. We aren't saved by our works. Works don't come first. Faith comes first and works follow, yet they are always tied together:

We are his workmanship, created in Christ Jesus for good works,
which God prepared beforehand, that we should walk in them.
EPHESIANS 2:10

Circle the reason Paul said we're created in Christ Jesus.

Underline what Paul said we should do as Christians.

Paul said we aren't saved *by* works, but we're saved *for* works. Works matter.

James said even demons know the truth about God. They could give all the right Sunday School answers. But they don't faithfully live for Him as Savior and Lord. They don't submit to His authority in their lives. Theirs is empty, dead faith. It's mere belief. Head knowledge doesn't save you. It doesn't make you a Christian. Doing this Bible study doesn't make you a Christian. Real faith is demonstrated in real action. Faith works.

Look back at the definition of *faith* you wrote at the beginning of today's personal study. Would you change anything? If so, cross out your original definition and write your new definition here.

Conclude your time of personal study by drawing near to God in faith through prayer. Thank Him for the gift of salvation through faith. Ask Him to help you live faithfully, boldly expressing your belief in Him through your actions.

PART 2: WORKS

What good is it, my brothers, if someone says he has faith but does not have works? Can that faith save him? If a brother or sister is poorly clothed and lacking in daily food, and one of you says to them, "Go in peace, be warmed and filled," without giving them the things needed for the body, what good is that? So also faith by itself, if it does not have works, is dead.
JAMES 2:14-17

The Book of James is like a commentary on the ministry of Jesus, applied to our lives as Christians. Let's rewind to the parable of the good Samaritan introduced last week. Jesus told a story of three men encountering another man who had been beaten, robbed, and left bleeding on the side of the road. The first two men were a priest and a Levite, highly respected religious figures in the Jewish community. But they failed to live out the essence of the law they taught others: love your neighbor as yourself. Their religion was worthless because what they claimed to believe in their minds didn't result in changed hearts and behaviors.

It was the Samaritan—one whom Jesus' original audience looked down on as inferior, a man with whom they wouldn't dare associate in their social or religious circles—who proved to be the hero of the story. He demonstrated a heart of compassion through his actions.

Read Luke 10:25-37. Describe in detail everything each person did.

Priest:

Levite:

Samaritan:

Jesus went into great detail about the ways the Samaritan showed mercy. He didn't settle for a generic gesture of well-being. He met tangible needs. He took specific action. The Samaritan not only tended to the man's wounds and took him to safety but also arranged for ongoing care and had a follow-up plan. The scenario makes it clear that the Samaritan had nothing to gain from his actions. He was traveling. He was in a dangerous area. It was an inconvenience that cost him time and resources and broke social norms. Yet he took action and did what he knew was right.

The men known for their devout religious service should have been the heroes of the story. Instead, they come off worse than the unknown robbers. Despite the countless other laws the religious men had kept (like supposedly never committing adultery or murder), they became transgressors of the whole law when they failed to love their neighbor (Jas. 2:8-13). They became the villains of the story, cold and heartless. Their faith was dead without works. It was the unassuming underdog who saved the day. Good works were needed to save this man in need.

Read Jesus' teaching about works and nonworks in Matthew 25:31-46.

What surprising connection did Jesus make between the way we treat other people and our relationship with Him?

How do you know Jesus wasn't teaching works-based salvation?

Don't misunderstand Jesus' point. The sheep weren't saved by their good works. They weren't trying to earn their way into heaven. In fact, they didn't even know they were doing these works for Jesus. They were just as surprised as the goats were when Jesus pointed out the works that had and hadn't been done for Him.

The sheep's good works were evidence of hearts that gladly served the King and loved the Father who had blessed them. They weren't trying to gain entry into His presence; rather, they were already living as citizens of the kingdom, fulfilling the royal law, loving their neighbors as themselves.

In this shocking parable the sin and faithlessness being judged aren't doing bad things but not doing the right things. The goats' nonworks revealed hearts that didn't truly know and love Jesus. They're what theologians call sins of omission (good works not done), as opposed to sins of commission (sinful works done).

Use the following table to reflect on specific ways you've been convicted, encouraged, and changed through this study of James so far. Follow the three prompts to complete the columns.

I BELIEVE. Identify commands or truths from Scripture about the Christian life that have been on your heart lately.

SO I WILL. Identify ways you can express faith through your actions.

AND I WON'T. Identify the opposite action or nonaction.

I believe ...	so I will ...	and I won't ...

What you truly believe will be evident in what you do and don't do. Pray for a constant awareness of the opportunities you have each day to practice pure and undefiled religion, fulfilling the royal law of Christlike love and remaining unstained by the world. Remind yourself of the truths identified in the chart: I believe _______, so I will _______, and I won't _______.

WEEK 6

BLESSINGS / CURSES

GROUP STUDY

START

Welcome everyone to the group. Take a minute to review Week 5 before starting Week 6.

Before starting new content, we'll take a few minutes to review the previous week, keeping in mind that the Christian life is one of transformation, not just information. The overarching message of James is that our faith expresses itself in our works.

FAITH. In what ways is your faith growing? What's one thing you learned through group discussion or personal study this past week?

WORKS. When did the message of James seem especially relevant this past week? How did you apply what you're learning to your daily life?

Last week we explored what our actions reveal about our faith. True, saving faith will be evident in our works. Works don't save us, but saving faith will be seen in our works. This week we're going to learn how this truth applies to our words. The words we speak reveal what's in our hearts.

How often do you imagine the average person speaks in a day?

Who thinks they speak more than the average person in a typical day? Who thinks they speak less than the average person?

We have countless opportunities throughout each day to use our words and to learn from our words. Today we'll discover how.

To prepare for the Week 6 video, pray that God will help each person understand and apply this truth:

Our words can be either a blessing or a curse to the people around us. Believers must learn to control their tongues and use their words for good, not evil.

WATCH

Use the space below to take notes
while you watch the Session 6 video.

1. Words are ____________________. With them we bless, we build up. With them we curse, we burn to the ground.

2. Words ______________ in ways that we really aren't even aware of.

3. Be careful who you __________________ to.

4. Words have defined _________________ for us.

5. Christianity spread not because in the first century we had magnificent ____________________, but rather because the __________ _______________ was powerfully at work among them.

6. Words reveal the progress of our _____________.

7. One of the principle marks of maturity is __________-____________________.

8. The work of taming the tongue takes us right into the epicenter of all that is wrong with us, namely our ________________.

9. Our _________________ reveal what's really going on in our ______________.

10. What drives your ______________ is your heart. What drives your heart is your ____________________.

11. You build your identity on anything other than Jesus Christ, your words will be __________________ or ______________________ or both.

ANSWERS: 1) powerful; 2) wound; 3) listen; 4) reality; 5) orators, Holy Spirit; 6) faith; 7) self-discipline; 8) hearts; 9) words, hearts; 10)mouth, identity; 11) hateful, boastful

DISCUSS

Use the following questions to guide your discussion of the video.

James gives three illustrations to communicate the power of the tongue:

1. Bits in horses mouths
2. Rudders on ships
3. A spark in the forest

If we put bits into the mouths of horses so that they obey us, we guide their whole bodies as well. Look at the ships also: though they are so large and are driven by strong winds, they are guided by a very small rudder wherever the will of the pilot directs. So also the tongue is a small member, yet it boasts of great things. How great a forest is set ablaze by such a small fire! And the tongue is a fire, a world of unrighteousness. The tongue is set among our members, staining the whole body, setting on fire the entire course of life, and set on fire by hell. For every kind of beast and bird, of reptile and sea creature, can be tamed and has been tamed by mankind, but no human being can tame the tongue. It is a restless evil, full of deadly poison.

JAMES 3:3-8

What point did these illustrations make about our speech? Which illustration stood out most vividly to you? Why?

How have you personally felt the destructive power of words? When have you hurt someone with your words?

How have you personally felt the power of words to bless? When have you comforted someone with your words?

Without thinking for very long, you can probably come up with several examples of things you wish you hadn't said. Likewise, you can probably remember other times where someone has encouraged you and given you strength. Our words have the power to bless and to curse.

Read James 3:9-12.

What point did these illustrations make about our speech?

How do words reveal the progress of our faith?

What remaining questions or comments do you have about the video teaching or discussion?

What was challenging, convicting, encouraging, or timely for your current circumstances?

We're going to take time to respond to these teachings from James with confession and prayer. First we'll consider what our words reveal about our hearts and confess that to one another. Then we'll pray for one another. We need to bring into the light what has been deep in our hearts and then encourage one another with the good news of the gospel and the healing truth of God's Word.

Get into small groups of two to four people for confession and prayer. If space allows, small groups may want to gather in different areas of the room for a designated time before coming back together as a large group.

Use the following questions to facilitate a time of confession.

What type of speech do you struggle with most (gossip, judgmental, sarcastic, jealous, prideful, etc.)?

Around what people or in what situations are you most likely to sin with your words?

How do your words reveal sin, fear, lack of faith, or other issues in your heart?

Ask the people in your group: What do you see as a blind spot in the way I speak? In what ways am I prone to show sin without knowing it?

Pray specifically for each person in your small group in response to his or her confession.

Return to the larger group for your usual time of prayer, sharing updates and new requests.

Close in prayer for the group.

PRAYER REQUESTS

PERSONAL STUDY

PART 1: BLESSINGS

In the beginning, God created the heavens and the earth. The earth was without form and void, and darkness was over the face of the deep. And the Spirit of God was hovering over the face of the waters. And God said, "Let there be light," and there was light. And God saw that the light was good. And God separated the light from the darkness. God called the light Day, and the darkness he called Night. And there was evening and there was morning, the first day.
GENESIS 1:1-5

The first thing we learn about God from Scripture is that He's the all-powerful (omnipotent), preexistent Creator. He made everything from nothing. Theologians call this creation *ex nihilo*. God didn't merely rearrange and shape matter into a more meaningful and increasingly complex reality. He created something—everything—from nothing.

How did God create the heavens and the earth? He spoke. Scripture portrays it as an overwhelmingly beautiful display of power and intimacy. Literally everything came into existence in obedience to God's direction. He orchestrated the heavens and the earth. Scripture affirms "all things" were created by, through, and for God the Son (Col. 1:16), while God the Holy Spirit completed, filled, and brought life to creation. Genesis 1 opens a subtle window into the relationships within the Trinity.

A beautiful rhythm emerges in the opening verses of the Bible. The phrase "God said" appears ten times in Genesis 1. Each day begins with "God said." Each day it God's word became reality. Over and over. God said, and it was so. God said, and it was so. The first day. The second day. The third day. It was good. It was good.

God gave names to His creation. He called the light day and the darkness night. He called the dry land earth and the waters seas. God spoke to creatures: "Be fruitful and multiply" (v. 22). God conversed with Himself, the triune Godhead: "Let us make man in our image" (v. 26). Finally, God spoke to the man and the woman, blessing them as unique among everything else He had spoken into existence.

Read Genesis 1, paying attention to God's words.

What words are used in Genesis 1 to indicate speech?

Why is it important to understand that God is both powerful and personal, transcendent yet intimate?

God has made Himself known to us. He has entrusted us with His Word. As image bearers and ambassadors of our King, we should be intentional about spreading the good news of reconciliation with our Creator (2 Cor. 5:11-21).

Your words are powerful. You can't speak stars and planets into existence, but you can speak in a way that spreads light or darkness.

Think about the most recent words you spoke to somebody. Were they generally positive or negative?

- ☐ **Positive**
- ☐ **Negative**

In general, would you consider your speech to be negative and discouraging or positive, encouraging, and life-giving? Mark your response on the scale.

1 2 3 4 5 6 7 8 9 10
Always negative **Always positive**

Your words and your tone of voice—what you say and how you say it—create an environment that's either more or less conducive to the gospel. What you say in general contributes to the likelihood that someone will listen to what you have to say specifically about abundant, eternal life through faith in Christ. The words of Proverbs are true:

Death and life are in the power of the tongue.
PROVERBS 18:21

It may seem dramatic to say that we have the power of life and death in our speech, but Scripture constantly warns about the power of our words. We can speak words that heal or that hurt; that are hopeful or hateful; that build up or tear down; that embody Christ, boast in self, or belittle others. James wrote:

From the same mouth come blessing and cursing.
My brothers, these things ought not to be so.
JAMES 3:10

Choose your words carefully. Will you bless or curse?

Read Hebrews 10:24-25. Why is encouragement an important part of Christian community?

Name some people to whom you can speak encouraging words of life. (Maybe you need to start by apologizing for negative words you've said.) Then note specific things you can say to encourage them to grow closer to God.

Close your time of study by praying for a strong awareness of the power of your words and of opportunities to encourage others. Thank God for making Himself known in Scripture and for entrusting you with the gospel. Ask for spiritual discernment in daily conversations.

Let no corrupting talk come out of your mouths,
but only such as is good for building up, as fits the
occasion, that it may give grace to those who hear.
EPHESIANS 4:29

PART 2: CURSES

Every kind of beast and bird, of reptile and sea creature, can be tamed and has been tamed by mankind, but no human being can tame the tongue. It is a restless evil, full of deadly poison. With it we bless our Lord and Father, and with it we curse people who are made in the likeness of God.
JAMES 3:7-9

Many people misunderstand the biblical concept of cursing. When the Bible condemns cursing, it's not addressing profanity. So-called bad words may be offensive and inappropriate, but poor manners may be more ignorant than sinful. However, a type of crude language is beyond rude:

Let there be no filthiness nor foolish talk nor crude joking, which are out of place, but instead let there be thanksgiving.
EPHESIANS 5:4

While crudeness may not appear to be as hateful on the surface as cursing, the root is similar. Crude joking and filthiness are derogatory, sexually explicit comments that disrespect other people.

The key to understanding what Scripture condemns as cursing is clearly stated in James 3:9. Cursing is a verbal attack, hatred, a violence of heart toward image bearers of our Creator. It's a dehumanization of someone else, elevating ourselves to a judge by condemning another person. The sin isn't a rude word but hatred for another human being created in the likeness of God. Ultimately, it's disrespect for God.

Likewise, crude and filthy speech, even in jokes, dehumanizes and objectifies other men or women, viewing them as things to be used, consumed, and discarded. Cursing and crudeness deny God's likeness in human beings.

In the verses at the top of the page, underline the phrase "people who are made in the likeness of God" (v. 9). How might the comments and jokes you've made over the past month harm or dehumanize people made in the image of God?

James didn't mince words. He strung together a series of metaphors to etch into our hearts and minds the reality that our words are shockingly powerful. He compared the tongue to a horse's bit (v. 3), a ship's rudder (v. 4), a fire's spark (v. 5), a deadly poison (v. 8), and a salty pond (v. 12).

These images highlight the fact that one tiny comment can have a wildly disproportionate, damaging effect. If you've ever seen news footage of wildfires like the ones that ravaged Tennessee, Colorado, and the entire West Coast in recent years, you have an idea of how destructive and out of control a single spark can become.

Just as environmental conditions contribute to the spread of a wildfire, a host of factors are at play each time you open your mouth to speak. One hateful word can destroy a fragile heart. One careless word can spark intense hurt that you never imagined. A wound is no less painful when it's inflicted unintentionally.

How have your wounds affected your view of your self-worth, the way you relate to other people, and the way you relate to God?

How are careless words spoken by Christians harmful to the reputation of the church and by extension—Jesus Christ?

Read Matthew 12:33-37. Let yourself feel the weight of Jesus' words. Summarize this warning in your own words.

You'll be held accountable for your words. Why? Jesus said, "Out of the abundance of the heart the mouth speaks" (v. 34). In other words, what drives your mouth is your heart. The problem isn't the words you say, but the heart that produces them. What drives your heart is your identity. Speech is a heart issue. That's why words are so powerful. You're telling people what you ultimately believe to be true about yourself, who they are, and what they're worth.

Read 1 John 3:15 and Matthew 5:21-26.

Evaluate your heart in light of Scripture.

When do you get angry? What does your answer reveal about your heart?

What type of sinful speech is most difficult to control (cursing, crudeness, boasting, lying, gossiping)? What does your answer reveal about your heart?

Whom have you recently spoken to in a way that tears down rather than builds up?

What person or people do you often find yourself speaking to or talking about in a sinful way?

Jesus taught that you should take hatred in your heart and your hurtful words so seriously that you stop in the middle of whatever you're doing—even worship—to go make amends, confessing your sin to whomever you've hurt. Continuing with the religious act without addressing sinful words and attitudes toward other people deceives your heart and is ultimately worthless (Jas. 1:26).

James knew this topic is vitally important to the church. Loving God and people with our speech is a definitive characteristic of the Christian life. Nothing destroys community and witness faster than sinful speech. Furthermore, when your words reveal a heart problem, ignoring that sin will eat away at you like cancer.

Prayerfully examine your heart, asking God to convict and forgive you of sinful attitudes revealed in your speech. Read Romans 12:9-21 and let God's Word speak to your heart. Intentionally seek reconciliation with people toward whom you harbor sin in your heart or have hurt with your words.

WEEK 7

FALSE WISDOM

TRUE WISDOM

GROUP STUDY

START

Welcome everyone to the group. Take a minute to review Week 6 before starting Week 7.

Before starting new content, we'll take a few minutes to review the previous week, keeping in mind that the Christian life is one of transformation, not just information. The overarching message of James is that our faith expresses itself in our works.

FAITH. In what ways is your faith growing? What's one thing you learned through group discussion or personal study this past week?

WORKS. When did the message of James seem especially relevant this past week? How did you apply what you're learning to your daily life?

This is the middle point in our study of James. This week's topic is essential in our Christian lives. Everything hinges on whether the standard by which we live is true or false.

To prepare for the Week 7 video, pray that God will help each person understand and apply this truth:

In living our lives, we can follow worldly wisdom that's false or godly wisdom that's true. We must examine every thought and deed by the Lord's truth, the Word, and by no other standard.

WATCH

Use the space below to take notes while you watch the Session 7 video.

1. God is for _______.

2. You are not the ____________.

3. You are not uppermost in His affections, because if you were, God would be an _____________________ Himself.

4. So, a _________________ in God that leads to a rejoicing in God frees up the soul in magnificent ways.

5. If God is for God, that means every command in the Bible leads me into ________.

6. God has designed the world to work in a specific way, leading to _________ glory and ________ joy.

7. False wisdom is marked by bitter ___________________ and selfish _________________, because you are all there is.

8. False wisdom is ________________, _________________, and ________________.

9. True wisdom is rooted in ___________________.

10. We grow in wisdom as we grow in _______________________ of the God of the Bible.

11. We grow in wisdom as we walk in ______________________.

12. God gives us godly _________________ to help us navigate what's wisdom and what's not.

13. True _____________ is found only in the person and work of Jesus Christ.

ANSWERS: 1) God; 2) point; 3) idolater; 4) delight; 5) joy; 6) God's, my; 7) jealousy, ambition 8) earthly, unspiritual, demonic; 9) eternity; 10) understanding; 11) community; 12) leaders; 13) wisdom

DISCUSS

Use the following questions to guide your discussion of the video.

We grow in wisdom as we:

1. Grow in understanding of the God of the Bible.
2. Grow in wisdom as we walk in community.

True wisdom is built on two foundational realities:

1. God is for God.
2. God has designed the world to work in a specific way.

Let's examine both foundations of true wisdom and contrast them with false wisdom.

"God is for God" means that God is radically God-centered. He seeks His own good and glory before He seeks ours. Why is this good for us?

False wisdom is essentially the opposite of true wisdom. False wisdom is marked by bitter jealousy and selfish ambition, because we see ourselves as the center.

False wisdom is:

1. Earthly
2. Unspiritual
3. Demonic

If God pursued our glory first, how would that make Him an idolater?

Why do people want to believe God pursues our glory before His own? Why would that ultimately be harmful for us?

Now think about what it means to say God has designed the world to work in a specific way.

Why should the way God designed the world concern us?

In what ways is this truth liberating? Give an example of how God's design of the world could affect a practical decision.

What's the opposite of this idea, according to worldly wisdom?

Why is it necessary to understand both of these realities in order to embrace true wisdom? What could happen if you accepted one of these as true but not the other?

How would you summarize the primary message of worldly wisdom?

Consider the statement:

The more your life is about you,
the more miserable you're going to be.

When and how have you experienced this to be true?

The wisdom of the world is rooted in selfishness. While our culture disciples us to believe our determination, our truth, and our happiness are the most important things in life—these ideas run contrary to God's Word. All people were meant to find their ultimate purpose and delight in God. True wisdom means we embrace God's vision of how the world works.

Who is wise and understanding among you? By his good conduct let him show his works in the meekness of wisdom. But if you have bitter jealousy and selfish ambition in your hearts, do not boast and be false to the truth. This is not the wisdom that comes down from above, but is earthly, unspiritual, demonic. For where jealousy and selfish ambition exist, there will be disorder and every vile practice. But the wisdom from above is first pure, then peaceable, gentle, open to reason, full of mercy and good fruits, impartial and sincere. And a harvest of righteousness is sown in peace by those who make peace.

JAMES 3:13-18

What are the characteristics of false wisdom? Which of these traits do you most struggle with?

What are the characteristics of true wisdom? Which have you seen the Spirit of God producing in your life?

What remaining questions or comments do you have about the video teaching or discussion?

What was challenging, convicting, encouraging, or timely for your current circumstances?

Close in prayer.

PRAYER REQUESTS

PERSONAL STUDY

PART 1: FALSE WISDOM

There is a way that seems right to a man,
but its end is the way to death.
PROVERBS 14:12

Two false beliefs drive all of your destructive behavior:

1. My life is about me. My happiness matters most.

2. No absolute, objective standard by which I must live. All people have the right to their own preferences and opinions about what will make them happy.

That's pretty much the mainstream view in today's culture, right?

Let the implications of those beliefs sink in for a moment. Approximately seven billion people live on the planet. Seven billion people can't all be right. Seven billion people can't all do whatever they want. Seven billion people can't all determine their own paths to finding personal happiness. Seven billion people can't be at the center of the universe. This is a chaotic impossibility. And we know it's impossible, but we love the lie.

Think about your day. In what ways are you exposed to the message of self-centered happiness? Each time you recognize this empty philosophy, remind yourself of Proverbs 14:12.

These lies sum up our cultural philosophy and the root of sin, pride, and selfishness. We see these lies all the way back in the garden of Eden when Adam and Eve decided they wouldn't trust their Creator. *Surely,* they reasoned, *there must be something better than what God has designed.* So they reached out and took what God had told them would destroy them.

Here's the cruel irony: the more life is about you, the more miserable you'll be.

How sick and twisted are we, knowing we can never make ourselves happy apart from God, yet constantly trying to do so? We're like Adam and Eve, hiding from the Creator behind a tree He created, as if He won't see us. We doubt His goodness and His sufficiency.

We think:

> *Maybe He's holding out on us. Maybe I should take that bite. Maybe I should choose for myself. Maybe I'd be better at running my own life than the God who created the entire universe. Maybe life isn't about God. Maybe life is about me. Maybe God should be all about me too. If I'm going to believe in God, it will be on my own terms. I can't believe in a God who doesn't do things the way I would do them. I can't believe in a God who doesn't always make me happy. After all, the ultimate standard in life is my own happiness.*

For each of the following areas of your life, list some ways you act from self-interest.

God:

Education:

Work:

Sports/Activities:

Family:

Friendships:

Money:

Time:

Home:

Church:

Your beliefs, philosophies, and attitudes affect your life. Your inner thought life spills over into your daily life. True wisdom will prove itself in meekness and good works. False wisdom will result in "disorder and every vile practice" (Jas. 3:16).

In the following verses, draw a box around the three words used to describe false wisdom.

Who is wise and understanding among you? By his good conduct let him show his works in the meekness of wisdom. But if you have bitter jealousy and selfish ambition in your hearts, do not boast and be false to the truth. This is not the wisdom that comes down from above, but is earthly, unspiritual, demonic. For where jealousy and selfish ambition exist, there will be disorder and every vile practice.

JAMES 3:13-16

When you read these descriptions of false wisdom do they seem like an exaggeration to you? Why can't you afford to underestimate the affects of false wisdom?

How would the selfish mentality of false wisdom unavoidably lead to bitterness, jealousy, disorder, and vile practices?

Previously, James shocked readers by pointing out that even demons know the truth about God (2:19). Then, he emphasized that living outside God's design is demonic at its core. To deny that life is ultimately about God and is found by trusting Him and living according to His design isn't just shortsighted. It's pure evil.

Confess any areas of your life in which you've been living by false wisdom with self-centered purposes. Thank God for the forgiveness and new life made possible by surrendering your will to Christ as Lord. Ask for a heart and a mind focused on God's goodness and trustworthiness.

PART 2: TRUE WISDOM

Who is wise and understanding among you? By his good conduct let him show his works in the meekness of wisdom.
JAMES 3:13

True wisdom is inseparable from good conduct. Faith works. Wisdom acts.

Your actions reveal what you truly believe, just as words are the fruit born from whatever is rooted deep in your heart. This is a dominant theme of James' epistle. You've already encountered this foundational truth in James 1:22; 2:14-26.

The question remaining is whether the beliefs guiding your actions are fundamentally false (worldly) or true (godly). You'll examine worldliness and godliness even further next week. This week you need to clearly identify the foundation on which you're building your life—lies or truth.

It's easy to deceive yourself into thinking you've checked off all the right theological boxes, believing the right things about Jesus but continuing to live according to a worldview that's just like everybody else around you.

If a new student began attending your school, would she see a difference between your life as a believer and the lives of nonbelieving students? Other than attending church, are you generally the same as your classmates?

- ☐ **No difference**
- ☐ **Some difference**
- ☐ **Clearly different**

What's true wisdom? If two people's lives appear similar or if godless people seem more successful by worldly standards (Ps. 73:3), how do we define true wisdom? Jesus, like James, used images to illustrate true wisdom. In one famous parable, Jesus contrasted a wise man and a foolish man, two neighbors who appeared similar on the surface.

As you read the following parable, underline the basic definitions of wisdom and foolishness.

Everyone then who hears these words of mine and does them will be like a wise man who built his house on the rock. And the rain fell, and the floods came, and the winds blew and beat on that house, but it did not fall, because it had been founded on the rock. And everyone who hears these words of mine and does not do them will be like a foolish man who built his house on the sand. And the rain fell, and the floods came, and the winds blew and beat against that house, and it fell, and great was the fall of it.
MATTHEW 7:24-27

Using the opening line of Jesus' parable, write a simple definition.

Wisdom is ____.

Luke's Gospel includes this question from Jesus:

Why do you call me "Lord, Lord," and not do what I tell you?
LUKE 6:46

Let those words sink in. The term *Lord* means master. It's a term of respect and authority. But Jesus isn't interested in empty lip service. If you confess Jesus as Lord, then you should honor Him through obedience.

The homes of the wise man and the foolish man probably looked similar from the outside. The men could have been neighbors. The wisdom wasn't in the location. The wisdom was in the foundation. The foolish man never got below the surface. He settled for what people could easily see. The other man was willing to put in the work of obedience, digging deep to find a trustworthy foundation. That's wisdom.

What habits are you developing to move past surface-level lip service to Jesus and build a foundation of hearing and obeying His Word?

Fill in the blanks to complete James' description of wisdom.

"The wisdom from above is first ______________, then ______________, _______________, open to ________________, full of _______________ and good fruits, ________________ and ________________" (Jas. 3:17).

Notice that each characteristic of wisdom from above describes "good conduct," as James mentioned in verse 13. True wisdom isn't an ethereal, abstract concept. It's tangible. It's concrete. It's measurable. It's practical.

How does each of these traits demonstrate a foundational trust in God?

Pure:

Peaceable:

Gentle:

Open to reason:

Full of mercy:

Impartial:

Sincere:

Life isn't about you. God's activity doesn't revolve around you. God is for God. He has designed life to work a certain way. True wisdom embraces these realities as good and joyful. End your time of study by prayerfully reflecting on the words of this hymn.

When we walk with the Lord in the light of His Word,
What a glory He sheds on our way! Let us do His good will;
He abides with us still, and with all who will trust and obey.
Trust and obey, for there's no other way
To be happy in Jesus, but to trust and obey.[1]

1. John H. Sammis, "Trust and Obey," *Baptist Hymnal* (Nashville: LifeWay Worship, 2008), 500.

WEEK 8
WORLDLINESS
GODLINESS

GROUP STUDY

START

Welcome everyone to the group. Take a minute to review Week 7 before starting Week 8.

Before starting new content, we'll take a few minutes to review the previous week, keeping in mind that the Christian life is one of transformation, not just information. The overarching message of James is that our faith expresses itself in our works.

FAITH. In what ways is your faith growing? What's one thing you learned through group discussion or personal study this past week?

WORKS. When did the message of James seem especially relevant this past week? How did you apply what you're learning to your daily life?

This week we'll build on our previous study of true and false wisdom. Worldliness and godliness are both the root and the fruit of the wisdom we live by. False wisdom is rooted in and reproduces more worldliness. True wisdom is rooted in and produces more godliness.

To prepare for the Week 8 video, pray that God will help each person understand and apply this truth:

Our passions and desires are at war within us, and we must fight against them. Pride, boasting, and divisiveness mark worldly people, while humility, obedience, and repentance mark godly people.

WATCH

Use the space below to take notes while you watch the Session 8 video.

1. The quarrels that occur have everything to do with ______; it is not circumstantial, it is internally a _________________ reality.

2. People by the __________ of God are aware of the _________________ of God in their lives.

3. Gladness fuels ____________________ that fuels gladness.

4. If you feel as though you are entitled, you grow not in gratitude and gladness, but _________________.

5. You don't want God to give you what you ________________.

6. Friendships are ___________________ because you can't go deep with everyone.

7. God is not jealous ____________ you, he is jealous _________ you, for his own glory.

8. We submit by __________________ the devil.

9. "The ______________ made me do it" doesn't fly.

10. We submit by __________________ God.

11. We submit to God by taking __________ seriously.

ANSWERS: 1) you, spiritual; 2) grace, goodness; 3) gratitude; 4) contempt; 5) deserve; 6) restrictive; 7) about, for; 8) resisting; 9) devil; 10) pursuing; 11) sin

DISCUSS

Use the following questions to guide your discussion of the video.

What causes quarrels and what causes fights among you? Is it not this, that your passions are at war within you? You desire and do not have, so you murder. You covet and cannot obtain, so you fight and quarrel. You do not have, because you do not ask. You ask and do not receive, because you ask wrongly, to spend it on your passions. You adulterous people! Do you not know that friendship with the world is enmity with God? Therefore whoever wishes to be a friend of the world makes himself an enemy of God. Or do you suppose it is to no purpose that the Scripture says, "He yearns jealously over the spirit that he has made to dwell in us"? But he gives more grace. Therefore it says, "God opposes the proud but gives grace to the humble."

JAMES 4:1-6

When we get into an argument with someone, our tendency is often to blame the person we're arguing with before examining our own hearts.

The way we view the world causes us to grow in one of two ways:

1. Gladness and gratitude
2. Entitlement and contempt

Of the two ways people grow, which way are you growing?

What circumstances in life lead you to feel most entitled? Why should you find satisfaction in God regardless of your circumstances?

When we learn to spot God's goodness in our lives it leads to an ever-increasing sense of gladness and gratitude. As joy and satisfaction begin to grow in our lives, we learn to appreciate God's work regardless of circumstances. On the other hand, if we feel like God owes us something, instead of growing in gladness and gratitude, we will grow in contempt. The only thing we deserve from God is death and eternal punishment, but by His grace, He has given us life.

How does social media lead us to be entitled and ungrateful?

Matt described real friendship as rich, good, something to fight for, restrictive, and invites critique from God and others. How does this kind of friendship keep us from entitlement and worldliness?

Submit yourselves therefore to God. Resist the devil, and he will flee from you. Draw near to God, and he will draw near to you. Cleanse your hands, you sinners, and purify your hearts, you double-minded. Be wretched and mourn and weep. Let your laughter be turned to mourning and your joy to gloom.

JAMES 4:7-9

What three actions for submitting to God are commanded in these verses?

1. Resist the devil (v. 7).

What does it look like in practical terms to resist the devil? How are you establishing support systems and accountability to help you resist spiritual attack and temptation?

What has been most effective in helping you resist temptation at different times in your life?

2. Pursue God (v. 8).

What does it mean to draw near to God? For Him to draw near to you?

What practical steps do you currently take to structure your day or week to pursue God?

What has been most effective in helping you grow in your love for God?

3. Take sin seriously (vv. 1-6,8-9,10-12).

In what ways were you convicted and encouraged by the previous group session's time of confession and prayer? Did it encourage you to mourn sin and help you be more humble this week before God and your brothers and sisters in Christ?

What remaining questions or comments do you have about the video teaching or discussion?

What was challenging, convicting, encouraging, or timely for your current circumstances?

Close in prayer.

PRAYER REQUESTS

PERSONAL STUDY

PART 1: WORLDLINESS

What causes quarrels and what causes fights among you?
Is it not this, that your passions are at war within you?
JAMES 4:1

If you've ever been in a bookstore, you've seen the massive space dedicated to self-help or self-improvement. You may have even seen books classified as Christian self-help. But here's the reality. You can't help yourself. You're broken. Apart from Christ you're spiritually dead. You can't improve on death and brokenness. This is a bigger deal than not living up to your potential or settling for good instead of great. This is a matter of life or death.

The apostle Paul described the inner turmoil, the war within, like this:

I do not understand my own actions. For I do
not do what I want, but I do the very thing I hate.
ROMANS 7:15

What sin do you keep committing even though you hate it?

Worldly desires keep rearing their ugly heads in our lives. They're like zombies that chase after us, popping out of the shadows—a dead nature that won't quit. Don't pretend you can't relate to Paul's bold confession. You have to feel the gravity of the dead weight to experience freedom from this burden.

Read about the ongoing battle that rages inside us and the victory we share in Romans 7:15–8:11.

How would you summarize the problem we face as human beings (Rom. 7:15-25)?

How would you summarize our hope and means of victory (Rom. 8:1-11)?

There's no middle ground here. On the one hand you have sin, flesh, hostility, and death. On the other hand you have submission, the Holy Spirit, freedom, and life. You have nothing good inside you apart from Christ. You cannot become a better you simply by trying. You're naturally hostile toward God. An enemy.

Even though passions are at war within you, you're in Christ, and the same Spirit who raised Jesus from the dead is now within you. Now you've been set free from condemnation. Let's pause there for a moment. If you're in Christ, there's no condemnation. None. Not only have you been pardoned from the eternal death sentence that justice rightly demands, but you've also received the Spirit of Christ and His righteousness in the present.

If you're beating yourself up, carrying the weight of guilt and shame for your past, stop it. If you're judging yourself for the temptation and worldliness that creep up on you, stop it. There's no condemnation in the future or the present. You're free.

Remember, you're miserable when you live for yourself. You can't be the center of your own life and utmost in your own affections. It's a recipe for disaster.

Let's take a personal inventory now, using James as our guide.

Read James 4:1-12.

What quarrels have you had recently?

When are you most likely to fight?

What do you covet, desiring something you're unable to obtain?

What are you selfishly asking God to give you?

In what ways do you look most like the world?

When do you justify worldly thinking?

What are you most prideful about?

How are you currently disobeying God?

How are you currently getting too close to the devil?

Whom do you sin against with your words?

These aren't just bad habits. Even though you don't always realize the spiritual warfare that's raging around you, a quick survey of your day reveals battles and strongholds. The good news is that the world is a defeated foe. Christ has conquered sin, death, and hell. And the power that raised Jesus from the dead lives in you.

Pray in confession, repentance, and gratitude to Christ for saving you from worldliness and condemnation. Commit to disciplining your mind to recognize and reject worldly desires and to love the true wisdom of God.

Do not be conformed to this world, but be transformed
by the renewal of your mind, that by testing you may discern
what is the will of God, what is good and acceptable and perfect.
ROMANS 12:2

PART 2: GODLINESS

If we're in a constant state of wrestling within ourselves, even though we know we've been set free and given abundant life in Christ, it's important for us to identify what a victorious lifestyle looks like. How do we know we're fighting the good fight?

Circle the two commands in this verse.

Submit yourselves therefore to God.
Resist the devil, and he will flee from you.
JAMES 4:7

Remember, earthly, unspiritual, and demonic wisdom opposes the authority and goodness of God (Jas. 3:15). True wisdom and saving faith are marked by obedience to God. So when we're talking about godliness, submitting to God and resisting the devil are two sides of the same coin.

Submitting to God and resisting the devil are active postures. Godliness isn't passive. It's not blissful ignorance. Godliness is bowing to the King and holding your ground against the enemy. It's wrestling and standing firm in Christ even as the fiery darts of Satan aim to kill you.

Read Ephesians 6:10-18.

What's the source of your strength in spiritual warfare?

Why is it important to remember your struggles are spiritual?

What are the pieces of armor? What do they reveal about godliness?

What's the only offensive weapon described? What does it reveal about godliness?

Why is prayer an essential practice for godliness? In this passage of Scripture, is prayer primarily focused on our own godliness? What can you learn about godliness from this final call to prayer?

Paul placed this description of spiritual warfare and the armor of God at the end of his letter to the Ephesians after he described a life of faith in general and godliness in human relationships specifically. Why? Because a spiritual dynamic is at play in every interaction we have with another person.

Who encourages you to stand firm in godliness?

How do godly friendships encourage you to pursue godliness?

How does Paul's description of spiritual warfare and the armor of God change the way you see other people and your daily life?

We've repeatedly compared the writings of James and Paul to highlight the harmony of their message about the Christian life: Genuine faith always bears the fruit of godliness in character and conduct. We aren't saved by our good works, but our good works are inseparable from salvation. Faith produces godliness.

James used another relational term to describe a godly posture in life. He warned us not to be friends with the world. He wasn't referring to casual friendship. The severity of this worldly posture draws harsh language to characterize the way it affects our relationship with God:

You adulterous people! Do you not know that friendship with the world is enmity with God? Therefore whoever wishes to be a friend of the world makes himself an enemy of God.
JAMES 4:4

James didn't mean we shouldn't interact with and have friends who aren't yet believers. James wasn't commanding us to just stay in the church. In the context of the chapter, he was warning against worldly desires. The apostle John wrote at length about this concept of friendship with the world in his first letter.

Read 1 John 2:15-17 and summarize the relationship between godliness and friendship with the world.

Godliness sees things correctly. Seeing life as God designed it—with everything in its correct order of priority—is liberating. Why give yourself to shallow, superficial things that can never satisfy you? It's most reasonable and in your best interest to give yourself wholly to the One who created you and redeemed you. He has proved that He knows, desires, and acts on behalf of what's best for you. Godliness is marked by humility, obedience, and repentance, not selfishly chasing the fleeting desires of the world and your flesh. It's trusting that God is good. Focus your affections on the one true God who has relentless love for you.

Conclude your time of personal study by praising God. Draw near to Him by confessing your sin, admitting your dependence on Him, and expressing your love for Him. Humble yourself before Him by exalting Him, giving Him rightful praise and glory above everything else in your life. Spend time focusing on His wisdom and goodness.

WEEK 9

ARROGANCE/HUMILITY

GROUP STUDY

START

Welcome everyone to the group. Take a minute to review Week 8 before starting Week 9.

Before starting new content, we'll take a few minutes to review the previous week, keeping in mind that the Christian life is one of transformation, not just information. The overarching message of James is that our faith expresses itself in our works.

> **FAITH. In what ways is your faith growing? What's one thing you learned through group discussion or personal study this past week?**

> **WORKS. When did the message of James seem especially relevant this past week? How did you apply what you're learning to your daily life?**

This week we'll continue in the Book of James, moving from wordliness and godliness to arrogance and humility. James' themes naturally progress as one thought leads to the next. Last week James commanded us to resist the devil, pursue God, and take our sin seriously, humbling ourselves before God. Now we'll apply this perspective of humility to the way we live godly lives.

To prepare for the Week 9 video, pray that God will help each person understand and apply this truth:

Our view of the future greatly influences where we place our assurance. James urges us to humbly view all of our days as being under the sovereign will of the Lord.

WATCH

Use the space below to take notes while you watch the Session 9 video.

1. Any ground for boasting or swagger or self-exaltation is ________________.

2. If you know that you are ______________, then are you actually humble?

3. Most people don't think they are __________________. They just think they're good at what they do.

4. We pursue humility by understanding and acknowledging our __________________.

5. Not everyone is ________________.

6. When you refuse to enter in, when you refuse to be a part, you weaken yourself and you weaken ______ _____ _____.

7. To grow in humility, you have to stay _____________.

8. Curiosity is a ________________ acknowledgment that you don't know something.

9. If you want to pursue humility, learn to acknowledge _____________.

10. Our faith isn't a privatized, pulled-out, separated-out idea over here, but is integrated into ______________________ we do and all that we consider and all that we set our minds and hearts to.

11. If you're not doing what you know is right, that's still _____________

ANSWERS: 1) foolish; 2) humble; 3) arrogant; 4) weaknesses; 5) everything; 6) all of us; 7)curious; 8) playful; 9) others; 10) everything; 11) sin

DISCUSS

Use the following questions to guide your discussion of the video.

In what ways does the worldly, false wisdom of our culture promote arrogance? How is arrogance openly encouraged today? How are arrogance and self-centeredness subtly encouraged?

Come now, you who say, "Today or tomorrow we will go into such and such a town and spend a year there and trade and make a profit"—yet you do not know what tomorrow will bring. What is your life? For you are a mist that appears for a little time and then vanishes. Instead you ought to say, "If the Lord wills, we will live and do this or that." As it is, you boast in your arrogance. All such boasting is evil.

JAMES 4:13-16

Is it arrogant to make plans? Is it worldly to make a profit? What is James saying in these verses?

What was James' point in comparing us to a mist or a vapor? Why is this truth an important reality to keep in mind?

In building on the theme of true, godly wisdom, what else do we need to keep in mind about who we are in relation to who God is?

In what way is humility ultimately a posture of faith?

Matt identified three ways to pursue humility, as well as ways to test whether we're walking in arrogance.

1. We must understand and acknowledge our weaknesses.

Why is admitting weaknesses freeing? Why is acknowledging humility vital to the unity of the church?

Are you more prone not to recognize your own weakness or to feel that God can't use you because of your weaknesses? Why are both of these extremes really two sides of the same coin of arrogance?

2. We must stay curious.

Matt said curiosity is "a playful acknowledgment that you don't know something." Why do most people lack enough humility to admit they don't know something?

3. We must learn to acknowledge others.

In what way is acknowledging others connected to admitting our own weaknesses?

How do being opinionated and making ourselves the hero damage relationships?

In what ways are arrogance and pride at the heart of all sin?

How would you explain the nature of sin in one sentence or phrase?

So whoever knows the right thing to do and fails to do it,
for him it is sin.
JAMES 4:17

How does this verse expand our understanding of sin?

How does the cross give hope to those of us who haven't done the right thing? How does that hope lead us to humility?

What remaining questions or comments do you have about the video teaching or discussion?

What was challenging, convicting, encouraging, or timely for your current circumstances?

Close in prayer.

PRAYER REQUESTS

PERSONAL STUDY

PART 1: ARROGANCE

Arrogance in our lives can be obvious, but more subtle forms of arrogance are usually more dangerous to our souls. In this section James uncovers a harmful form of arrogance lurking in our hearts.

In these verses underline key words that signal a posture of arrogance.

Come now, you who say, "Today or tomorrow we will
go into such and such a town and spend a year there and trade
and make a profit"—yet you do not know what tomorrow will bring.
What is your life? For you are a mist that appears for a little time
and then vanishes. Instead you ought to say, "If the Lord wills,
we will live and do this or that." As it is, you boast in your arrogance.
All such boasting is evil. So whoever knows the right thing
to do and fails to do it, for him it is sin.

JAMES 4:13-17

Summarize the mentality being condemned in this passage.

What's the difference between open arrogance and hidden arrogance? Which is James describing here?

Give an example of each type.
Open arrogance:

Hidden arrogance:

Where does each show up in your life? Why are both dangerous?

This passage is more about the implicit (hidden) attitude of arrogance than the explicit (open) action. It's not literally evil to make plans or to do business. Countless Scriptures encourage wisdom in handling finances and responsibilities.

The warning here is against the false wisdom, worldly ambition, and self-centered confidence in believing that life revolves around you and that you have everything figured out. The sins in this passage are self-reliance and a lack of submission to the will of our sovereign God. This sin is declaring yourself to be sovereign. This involves believing the serpent's lie.

In what areas do you need to trust God and rely on His guidance and provision over your desires?

Read Genesis 3:1-7.

Why is questioning God an expression of arrogance?

When do you question whether God's Word should apply to you or whether an exception should be made?

The first sin resulted from the idea that man and woman had the right to question God. That subtle subversion of God's good, rightful authority put us on shaky ground, wavering on self-destruction.

It's important to note that in this account of the first temptation, it wasn't sensual desire that enticed Eve and then Adam.

Read Genesis 2:9. What words are used to describe every tree?

Read Genesis 3:6. What's the only way the forbidden fruit was different?

What does the original description of the garden reveal about God's goodness and about His desire for us?

What does the draw of the forbidden fruit reveal about the core of sin?

Beauty and pleasure are God's good gifts to us. They're part of His perfect design as the Creator. We refer to the blessings everyone can enjoy as common graces—natural beauty, pleasure for the senses, and good food, for example. Even the person most violently opposed to God's sovereign rule can enjoy these things to a degree. However, Christians experience common graces as good gifts from an even greater giver of the gift. The pleasure fuels humble gratitude. In contrast, the pleasure of an arrogant heart ends with itself as it consumes common graces without gratitude.

The original sin came from a desire to be self-sovereign. It challenged the sufficiency of God's sovereignty. The lie we all fall for is that we have the ability and the right to determine what we'll do with our lives without experiencing the consequence of death. The sin of being self-sovereign is taking our lives into our own hands and believing we can be in control.

We want to be like God. We want to choose what's right or wrong for ourselves. We don't want to believe His wisdom should be the standard we live by. He isn't good enough. We deserve more. We can have something better.

Review James 4:13-17, keeping in mind the temptation, sin, and consequence of Genesis 3:1-7. Use these Scriptures to guide a time of prayer in which you confess areas of self-sovereignty in your life, surrender control, and submit to God's gracious design for your life.

PART 2: HUMILITY

Our view of the future greatly influences where we place our assurance. Let's start by establishing a general idea of the way you view the future.

How often do you think about the future?

1 2 3 4 5 6 7 8 9 10
Never **Obsessively**

How often do you pray about the future?

1 2 3 4 5 6 7 8 9 10
Never **Obsessively**

What's your general attitude toward the future?

1 2 3 4 5 6 7 8 9 10
Fearful **Excited**

How much do your thoughts about the future affect your daily life?

1 2 3 4 5 6 7 8 9 10
Not at all **Consume everything**

What word would you use to describe your attitude toward the future?

When thinking about the future, what do you focus on?

What general conclusions can you come to, based on your previous answers?

The teaching in James 4:13-17 on a humble posture toward the future is thoroughly rooted in Jewish thinking about God's sovereignty. This perspective on time and the character of God was established from the very beginning. We see it in the creation of the world and in the law that first governed God's people, the Hebrews.

Read Exodus 20:8-11. Summarize the commandment and the reason given for it.

In what way is practicing a day of Sabbath rest an act of humility? What does keeping the Sabbath say about God's character?

Resting in God isn't a just rule to follow; it's an intentional act of humility, dependence, trust, and obedience. The Sabbath is an act of worship that declares faith in God's provision and sufficiency. We can take a break. Our lives don't depend on our own effort. In our culture, which wears busyness as a badge of honor and importance, it's likely that you need to evaluate your own practice of Sabbath rest. Do you really trust that if God can create the universe in six days, you can rest from the work He has given you to do?

Read Psalm 8. What humbling realities are emphasized?

What conclusion did the psalmist come to in his posture of humility?

Jesus also used illustrations from creation to put our anxious ambitions and concerns into perspective.

Read Matthew 6:25-33. Record the examples from nature that Jesus used to demonstrate God's sovereign care and what they teach us.

Jesus said worrying is an act of faithless pride that's characteristic of pagans who don't have a personal relationship with the sovereign Creator.

What does a life of humility look like? It obviously doesn't include a high view of yourself. You're not God. But it's also not a low view of yourself. You're a precious creation of God. It's not a lack of hard work. It's a healthy balance and a right view of why you work, how much you work, and what you're working for. It's ultimately trusting that God is in control and that you can live according to His sovereign design for your life and this world rather than believing you can take care of yourself:

Seek first the kingdom of God and his righteousness,
and all these things will be added to you.
MATTHEW 6:33

Your Creator and Heavenly Father loves you perfectly. He knows what you need. Among everything He has made, He has chosen to have a special relationship with you. The Book of Job contains a poetic conversation in which the Creator reminded Job, a man he loved deeply, that His power and wisdom were infinitely greater than limited human understanding (Job 38–41). When you're tempted to assume the position of self-sovereign in your life, these words are convicting, but when you humbly bow before God as Job did, they're deeply comforting.

Read Job 38–41 to catch a glimpse of God's overwhelming majesty and sovereignty over creation. Find a place where you can view the complexity of nature and worship your Creator with a sense of awe and reverence. Thank God for His sovereignty over every part of your life.

WEEK 10

OPPRESSOR/LABORER

GROUP STUDY

START

Welcome everyone to the group. Take a minute to review Week 9 before starting Week 10.

Before starting new content, we'll take a few minutes to review the previous week, keeping in mind that the Christian life is one of transformation, not just information. The overarching message of James is that our faith expresses itself in our works.

FAITH. In what ways is your faith growing? What's one thing you learned through group discussion or personal study this past week?

WORKS. When did the message of James seem especially relevant this past week? How did you apply what you're learning to your daily life?

Last week James warned against the danger of arrogance, calling Christians to live humbly, with a right perspective on themselves and God. He gave the examples of boasting about business plans and traveling to make a great profit. Plans aren't a problem. Profit isn't a problem. However, pride is a deadly problem.

"Come now," the writer said in James 4:13. He starts this week's warning the same way. James calls us to look closely at our lives as he digs deeper into the money-hungry pride that's a worldly stain on a person's heart.

To prepare for the Week 10 video, pray that God will help each person understand and apply this truth:

James warns the rich who oppress and exploit the underprivileged that riches will amount to nothing in the end. However, the humble and righteous will prevail.

WATCH

Use the space below to take notes while you watch the Session 10 video.

1. Money is ________________.

2. The heart is __________________.

3. A love of money is _______________.

4. Only the ________________ can deliver us from this.

5. The lie we will give our lives to is that we need ____________ of what we actually already _____________.

6. Money is so dangerous because you have ______________ in the wrong thing.

7. Your _______________ is a gracious gift from God to help you understand what's actually going on in you.

8. We use wealth to kind of create ________________ and as a ______________ to buffer us from life's anxieties.

9. Almost all crime is built upon ____________.

10. We are ________________, so the __________________ can never satisfy.

11. The whole basis of the gospel is rooted in the _________________ of God.

12. We've not just been saved ____________; we've been saved ______.

13. We need to grow in __________________ wisdom.

14. We have to pursue ___________________.

15. Be ________________.

ANSWERS: 1) dangerous; 2) deceptive; 3) deadly; 4) gospel; 5) more, have; 6) trusted; 7) wallet; 8) safety, shield; 9) money; 10) eternal, temporary; 11) generosity; 12) from, to; 13) financial; 14) contentment; 15)generous

DISCUSS

Use the following questions to guide your discussion of the video.

What was your first reaction when you realized we'll talk about money in this session? Why do you think you reacted that way? Why is money a sensitive subject for most people?

Scripture takes the subject of money very seriously. What we do with money and the degree to which we desire it may reveal our hearts more than our words and actions combined.

How does money offer a way to look into our hearts?

Everyone in this room is among the wealthiest people on the planet. This wealth is a tremendous blessing, but it also comes with great responsibility and risk.

Come now, you rich, weep and howl for the miseries that are coming upon you. Your riches have rotted and your garments are moth-eaten. Your gold and silver have corroded, and their corrosion will be evidence against you and will eat your flesh like fire. You have laid up treasure in the last days. Behold, the wages of the laborers who mowed your fields, which you kept back by fraud, are crying out against you, and the cries of the harvesters have reached the ears of the Lord of hosts. You have lived on the earth in luxury and in self-indulgence. You have fattened your hearts in a day of slaughter. You have condemned and murdered the righteous person. He does not resist you.

JAMES 5:1-6

How would you describe the emotional tone of these verses? Why do you think the message calls for such emotion?

Describe the situation addressed in these verses. How might we be prone to misunderstand James' message? What's actually being condemned here? What's isn't being condemned?

Let's discuss the four points Matt used to summarize this text and biblical wisdom about money.

1. Money is dangerous.

What's the distinction between money being dangerous and money being bad? How did the comparison to fire help clarify this point?

2. The heart is deceptive.

Why is this true not only for money but also for every area of our lives?

3. A love of money is deadly.

Why is discontentment toxic for our souls?

4. Only the gospel can deliver us.

How do we find contentment in the gospel? How do we find generosity at the heart of the gospel?

Matt explained that he and his wife, Lauren, have a generosity line item in their household budget that's a fun, disciplined way to develop a healthy intentionality in the way they use their money. He also mentioned his personal conviction about his local church, gospel ministry, and giving and living missionally.

How might these examples help you examine your own spending?

What has proved effective or helpful in your life for developing godly hearts and habits in regard to your finances?

What has proved effective or helpful in your life for developing godly hearts and habits in regard to your spending?

What remaining questions or comments do you have about the video teaching or discussion?

What was challenging, convicting, encouraging, or timely for your current circumstances?

Close in prayer.

PRAYER REQUESTS

PERSONAL STUDY

PART 1: OPPRESSOR

Come now, you rich, weep and howl for the miseries that are coming upon you. Your riches have rotted and your garments are moth-eaten. Your gold and silver have corroded, and their corrosion will be evidence against you and will eat your flesh like fire. You have laid up treasure in the last days. Behold, the wages of the laborers who mowed your fields, which you kept back by fraud, are crying out against you, and the cries of the harvesters have reached the ears of the Lord of hosts. You have lived on the earth in luxury and in self-indulgence. You have fattened your hearts in a day of slaughter. You have condemned and murdered the righteous person. He does not resist you.

JAMES 5:1-6

Once again James' imagery is intentionally vivid. This book of the Bible doesn't require a lot of reading between the lines.

Highlight words in the previous passage that communicate emotional intensity.

At this point in his letter, James began wrapping up his commentary on wealth and the related worldly desires that inevitably lead to personal and relational ruin. The Book of James has often been called the Proverbs of the New Testament. Like Solomon, James addressed the same themes at multiple points throughout the book, each time applying God's wisdom from a different angle. He addressed wealth so often and so strongly because it's a problem for all of us.

What did James say about wealth or poverty in the following verses?

James 1:9-11

James 1:27

James 2:1-9

James 4:1-4

James 4:13-16

James 5:1-6

How would you summarize James' overall teaching on wealth?

James was specific in his condemnation. He didn't make a blanket statement against rich people. He warned his readers throughout the letter about the selfish desire for riches. In chapter 5 he condemned:

- the inevitable abuse of power and the oppression of people that result from a self-centered attitude toward wealth, believing it will provide security;
- the indulgent posture of being self-sovereign;
- wealth gained at the expense of others;
- valuing possessions over people.

The image of wages wrongfully withheld from workers (vv. 4-6) brings to mind the account of the first murder of a righteous person. After Adam and Eve were removed from the garden of Eden, we read about their two sons. Abel worked the field, while Cain tended the flocks.

In an act of jealous anger and selfish ambition, Cain murdered his brother. Sin had fractured family and work. And just as God had looked for Adam and Eve following their act of rebellion, the voice of God confronted the angry brother:

The LORD said, "What have you done? The voice of your brother's blood is crying to me from the ground."
GENESIS 4:10

Maybe you can distance yourself from this story, assuring yourself you would never murder anyone. But look at James' words:

Behold, the wages of the laborers who mowed your fields, which you kept back by fraud, are crying out against you, and the cries of the harvesters have reached the ears of the Lord of hosts.
JAMES 5:4

You don't want to be Cain, and you don't want to be the rich oppressor under God's judgment. The examples from Genesis and James show how destructive the desire for wealth can be for our souls.

How has your desire for money and things affected your spiritual life?

What precautions do you take to guard your heart against an unhealthy materialism?

What are you going to offer God when you stand in judgment—nice clothes, a fancy car, a big house, your bank accounts? Remember Jesus' words:

What will it profit a man if he gains the whole world and forfeits his soul? Or what shall a man give in return for his soul? For the Son of Man is going to come with his angels in the glory of his Father, and then he will repay each person according to what he has done.
MATTHEW 16:26-27

Pause for a moment and prayerfully consider the words of Jesus you just read. Confess any greed, dishonesty, or materialism in your life. Commit to make things right if you've cheated, stolen, or withheld anything from anyone. Ask God to give you a heart that stewards financial blessings for His glory, not your own.

PART 2: LABORER

James went to great lengths to warn the church about wealth's corrupting power. His words often echo the teachings of Jesus, specifically the Sermon on the Mount. Let's look at the passage immediately before the one you studied last week about humbly relying on God's provision rather than anxiously seeking material possessions and trying to meet our physical needs.

Do not lay up for yourselves treasures on earth, where moth and rust destroy and where thieves break in and steal, but lay up for yourselves treasures in heaven, where neither moth nor rust destroys and where thieves do not break in and steal. For where your treasure is, there your heart will be also.
MATTHEW 6:19-21

Jesus' teaching sounds a lot like the harsh condemnation of wealthy oppressors in James 5:1-6. However, in this portion of the Sermon on the Mount, Jesus did more than warn against the fleeting, fragile nature of earthly comforts. He provided insight into the nature of treasure and the motivation behind work.

Read Matthew 6:24 and restate Jesus' point in your own words.

How have you experienced the truth of Jesus' teaching in this verse?

What practical steps have you taken to make sure you're serving God and storing up treasures in heaven?

How can you serve God with the wealth He has given you?

God's Word is clear about our attitude toward wealth and worldly ambition. Yet it clearly teaches wealth itself isn't inherently evil. Serving wealth as our master is the problem. Storing up treasures means we're investing in that which will last into eternity: God's mission in the world. Much of what we pursue that leads to our glory and comfort here on earth won't serve us in eternity. Instead of using our material resources to build wealth here, we must build what will outlast this world and continue into the next.

Consider Paul's words about our work:

> *Whatever you do, work heartily, as for the Lord and not for men, knowing that from the Lord you will receive the inheritance as your reward. You are serving the Lord Christ.*
> COLOSSIANS 3:23-24

As students, some of you may work and others may not. But you all work *at* something. How would you describe the nature of your "work," whether it's a part-time job, or even school?

How can you use your current circumstances to work for the Lord?

What does it mean to "work heartily"? Why does the way we do our work, or work at school or extracurriculars, matter to God?

Work is a blessing God gave before the fall (Gen. 1:28-29; 2:8). Work became a burden only after the fall (Gen. 3: 17-19). The implications of this fact are enormous. God has created each of us to do deep, meaningful work. Our jobs aren't simply a means to provide for ourselves but to serve the Lord with our lives.

When we begin to see our work as a means to glorify God instead of a way to gain more for ourselves, our relationship with wealth and material possessions changes. From the Scriptures we can draw clear principles and specific applications for our own work situations.

Read Ephesians 6:5-9. How would you summarize the overarching principle about work?

What specific commands are given to servants that apply to those under authority?

What specific commands are given to masters that apply to leaders and anyone in a position of authority?

How does your work ethic need to change to better reflect the principles Jesus and Paul taught?

Close your time of personal study by dedicating your work to God. Ask for a fresh awareness of your heart's desires and ask God to help you focus entirely on spiritual treasures, not material possessions. Commit to use your work to serve the true Master, no matter what your employment situation may be.

WEEK 11

SUFFERING / COMFORT

GROUP STUDY

START

Welcome everyone to the group. Take a minute to review Week 10 before starting Week 11.

Before starting new content, we'll take a few minutes to review the previous week, keeping in mind that the Christian life is one of transformation, not just information. The overarching message of James is that our faith expresses itself in our works.

FAITH. In what ways is your faith growing? What's one thing you learned through group discussion or personal study this past week?

WORKS. When did the message of James seem especially relevant this past week? How did you apply what you're learning to your daily life?

In this week's passage, James turns his attention from warning the oppressors to comforting the ones who were suffering. Following his intense condemnation of people who put their hope in money, James pointed to our source of true hope.

To prepare for the Week 11 video, pray that God will help each person understand and apply this truth:

In times of suffering, believers are to endure with patience and steadfastness, keeping their eyes on the Lord. He's compassionate and merciful to His children in every circumstance.

WATCH

Use the space below to take notes while you watch the Session 11 video.

1. Persevering, ________-______________ faith in God requires patience.

2. Be ______________, the Lord is coming.

3. Be patient; God is accomplishing something in you.

4. God continues to lavish upon us ____________________ grace.

5. To understand the mercy that's been extended to us, enables us to _______________ mercy to others.

6. Be patient. God's promises are ___________.

7. The accuser is constantly asking ________________, and even when God grants permission, He gives _________________.

8. God has never ____________________ you.

9. Be patient with __________ _______________.

10. Nobody gets out of a ________________ _____ world unscathed.

ANSWERS: 1) glad-hearted; 2) patient; 3) accomplishing; 4) extravagant; 5) extend; 6) true; 7) permission, parameters; 8) betrayed; 9) each other; 10) Genesis 3

DISCUSS

Use the following questions to guide your discussion of the video.

James was writing to Christians who were likely externally oppressed and internally conflicted. His words of comfort address both situations. In fact, the two often go hand in hand, but sometimes we wrestle with one without the other.

How can external circumstances cause internal struggles? How can internal conflict spill out into external circumstances?

Currently, we all face some degree of struggle. Whether or not it's persecution or extreme suffering, we all struggle.

Are your current areas of stress and struggle primarily external, internal, or both? Explain.

In the video Matt highlighted five points of comfort and hope in James' message for believers who are suffering.

1. Be patient; the Lord is coming.

On a scale of 1 to 10, 1 being never and 10 being constantly, how often do you think about Jesus' return?

1 2 3 4 5 6 7 8 9 10

Never Constantly

Do you assume we're more or less likely to expect Jesus' return than James' original audience in the early church? Why?

Be patient, therefore, brothers, until the coming of the Lord. See how the farmer waits for the precious fruit of the earth, being patient about it, until it receives the early and the late rains. You also, be patient. Establish your hearts, for the coming of the Lord is at hand.
JAMES 5:7-8

In what way do these verses express a foundational truth for our Christian faith?

How do they give comfort, hope, and patience in real-life difficulties?

2. Be patient; God is accomplishing something in you.

How has God used suffering, oppression, struggle, and discipline to grow your relationship with Him and others?

Do not grumble against one another, brothers, so that you may not be judged; behold, the Judge is standing at the door.
JAMES 5:9

3. Be patient with one another.

How can we, as the church, greatly help or hurt one another while enduring difficulty?

How does keeping in mind that the Judge is at the door fuel our patience with one another?

4. Be patient; God's promises are true.

As an example of suffering and patience, brothers, take the prophets who spoke in the name of the Lord. Behold, we consider those blessed who remained steadfast. You have heard of the steadfastness of Job, and you have seen the purpose of the Lord, how the Lord is compassionate and merciful.

JAMES 5:10-11

Many men and women in the Bible experienced suffering. Which example is most encouraging and comforting to you? Why?

What are some of your favorite promises from God's Word? Why are they especially meaningful to you? When have you found much-needed comfort in God's Word?

5. Be patient with one another—seriously.

How does patience allow our faith to grow?

What remaining questions or comments do you have about the video teaching or discussion?

What was challenging, convicting, encouraging, or timely for your current circumstances?

Close in prayer.

PRAYER REQUESTS

PERSONAL STUDY

PART 1: SUFFERING

Be patient, therefore, brothers, until the coming of the Lord. See how the farmer waits for the precious fruit of the earth, being patient about it, until it receives the early and the late rains. You also, be patient. Establish your hearts, for the coming of the Lord is at hand. Do not grumble against one another, brothers, so that you may not be judged; behold, the Judge is standing at the door. As an example of suffering and patience, brothers, take the prophets who spoke in the name of the Lord. Behold, we consider those blessed who remained steadfast. You have heard of the steadfastness of Job, and you have seen the purpose of the Lord, how the Lord is compassionate and merciful.

JAMES 5:7-11

Circle the words *patient* and *patience* in the verses. How many times do they appear?

Unlike most people in our culture today, the early Christians likely expected Jesus to return during their lifetimes. Many believed He could return at any moment. Today anyone predicting Jesus' return is recognized as a false teacher (Mark 13:32), but at the time, the disciples had seen Jesus ascend into heaven and hoped He would return soon (Acts 1:11). In the New Testament church, waiting for the Lord's return sometimes led to unhealthy inactivity (1 Thess. 4:13–5:11), and today it can lead to unhelpful speculation and preoccupation. James mentioned the Lord's return as a means to encourage His audience to see their suffering in light of the bigger picture.

What words in this passage indicate that the Lord will return?

How should the certain return of the Lord affect the way you view your suffering?

For James' audience, the reality of Jesus' return wasn't a distraction that led to speculation, predictions, and false teachings. It was a source of comfort and hope in the midst of difficulty and suffering.

The word translated *coming* in our English Bibles was originally used to describe the arrival of a king. The repeated reminder to be patient was James' pastoral way of rightly focusing the believers' perspective on the suffering they were experiencing. The believers could patiently endure their suffering because Jesus would return as Savior and Judge.

Reread James 5:7-11.

What difficulty comes to mind when you read about the farmer waiting for rain? How can you relate?

What difficulty do you see in the warning against grumbling? How can you relate?

What difficulty do you see in the example of the prophets? How can you relate?

James opened his letter with the topic of suffering, and he closed his letter with a call for patience in suffering. It's a major theme of the book. James indirectly addressed forms of difficulty in His teaching on the other topics. A right view of wealth and poverty will relieve suffering. A right view of our faith in action will relieve suffering. A right use of our speech will relieve suffering. Suffering always happens in a context, and the ultimate context is God's sovereignty. Adopting God's perspective on suffering allows us to see it within His plan.

Look back at the beginning of the letter. How does addressing the readers as "the twelve tribes in the Dispersion" in James 1:1 set a context of suffering for the entire letter? What does this phrase refer to?

Consider another New Testament statement on suffering:

> *We do not lose heart. Though our outer self is wasting away, our inner self is being renewed day by day. For this light momentary affliction is preparing for us an eternal weight of glory beyond all comparison.*
> 2 CORINTHIANS 4:16-17

How is Paul's view of suffering similar to the view of suffering expressed in James?

When we're in the middle of suffering, why is patience so difficult to come by?

Suffering is for now but not forever. The Bible doesn't downplay the reality of suffering. It acknowledges all the ugliness and pain of this life, but it presses us toward hope. Because of Jesus, who willingly suffered to defeat suffering and death, the glory that lies ahead isn't worth comparing to the pain of the present. For the redeemed, comfort lies beyond our suffering.

What has helped you endure trials and difficulties? How can you help others who are suffering?

Close your time of personal study by praying for the ability to endure based on a rock-solid assurance that the Lord will return and right every wrong. Thank Him for His work in your life, even lessons, blessings, and opportunities that come to you through tears and pain.

PART 2: COMFORT

Here's one of the many great joys in believing that our God is sovereign: suffering isn't pointless. For believers in Christ, life is often tough, but it's never hopeless.

God is in control. The world isn't randomly and chaotically spinning out of control while we wait for Jesus to come back and take us out of here, flying us off to heaven before the whole thing crashes and burns. He's in control now—even in the pain and suffering. Jesus, the Son of God, is reigning and ruling at the right hand of the Father.

The false wisdom of the world insists that if God exists, His purpose must be to make us happy. However, the reality of suffering in the world blows the self-sovereign delusion out of the water.

Either God is powerless over suffering, indifferent to suffering, or sovereign over suffering. Jesus' resurrection proves God is powerful, loving, and sovereign over suffering, sin, and death. No human experience is wasted or meaningless—not even pain. God doesn't cause sin and evil, but He does control it (Jas. 1:12-18). God is present and working through it all.

Look at Paul's words:

> *We know that for those who love God all things work together for good, for those who are called according to his purpose.*
> **ROMANS 8:28**

Are all things good? No. Some things are truly painful and evil. But is God able to work in and through all things to accomplish His good purpose? Absolutely.

Consider the cross. The arrest, trial, beating, mockery, crucifixion, and murder of the Son of God were evil. It was the darkest moment in human history. The sky went dark, and the earth shook. It was pure evil. Yet it was simultaneously inseparable from God's gracious work to save sinners from eternal judgment in hell.

In Week 9 you prayerfully reflected on God's majestic creation, power, and wisdom as revealed in the story of Job. Before that description of God's sovereignty and power, Job suffered horrifically and received terrible counsel from his wife and friends. Essentially, they all said God was causing the suffering as judgment Job somehow brought on himself. His suffering was his fault.

What these people couldn't know was that Satan had to get God's permission even to touch Job (Job 1:9-12). Job's suffering wasn't caused by God, yet it was never beyond God's control. Job did nothing to bring suffering on himself, nor was it a sign of God's displeasure, indifference, or judgment. In fact, God was greatly pleased with Job's faithfulness and was confident Job would patiently endure the trial. God ultimately blessed and restored him.

Just because we may not understand our difficulty doesn't mean God isn't in control or that His good purposes won't be accomplished.

Read Isaiah 55:8-9. In what ways do you find God's declaration comforting?

How would you comfort someone with the wisdom in Isaiah 55:8-9?

Read 2 Corinthians 1:3-6. Summarize what Paul said about suffering and comfort.

Christians are able and expected to comfort one another. We extend hope to people who are hurting, empathizing with their pain and exalting Christ, our suffering Savior. We encourage one another to patiently endure, knowing our pain isn't wasted and God will ultimately use it for His good purpose.

Read James 5:7-12.

James' instruction to be patient was a word of comfort. It was a word of hope. It was a spiritual perspective that rightly framed the suffering and hardship of daily life on this earth. The words "Be patient" (v. 7) were strong yet gentle pastoral hands that lifted the weary heads of believers to fix their eyes on Jesus.

James concluded his thought on comfort and suffering by saying we should be people of our word (v. 12). We shouldn't try to assure people that we're trustworthy by swearing by things we can't control. Our speech should convey the integrity of the gospel. Our words can cause great harm or bring great healing. We should use them wisely.

What connection can be made between the encouragement in James 5:9,12 and suffering and comfort?

How does being people of our word allow us to serve and minister to others in distress?

James' use of the phrase "But above all" (v. 12) signals the conclusion of his argument. His advice about vows is related to his command not to grumble against one another. In the context of difficulty, we need to be patient with one another. It's much easier to extend patience to people who are gracious and dependable.

Life is challenging and difficult. Being trustworthy, patient, and willing to serve others and to point to help when we can't makes a significant impact on the way we live with one another in the body of Christ. The world puts enough pressure on us; we shouldn't put additional pressure on one another.

To whom do you need to extend grace this week? Whom do you need to serve?

When has someone's encouragement or presence been a source of comfort to you?

Conclude your personal study by praying that God will help you control your tongue and use it for His good purpose of bringing comfort and hope. Ask God to sovereignly provide opportunities to encourage others and to share the hope found in the gospel of Jesus Christ.

WEEK 12

FAITHFUL / FAITHLESS

GROUP STUDY

START

Welcome everyone to the group. Take a minute to review Week 11 before starting Week 12.

Before starting new content, we'll take a few minutes to review the previous week, keeping in mind that the Christian life is one of transformation, not just information. The overarching message of James is that our faith expresses itself in our works.

FAITH. In what ways is your faith growing? What's one thing you learned through group discussion or personal study this past week?

WORKS. When did the message of James seem especially relevant this past week? How did you apply what you're learning to your daily life?

James was reaching the end of his letter. The Scriptures we've studied over the past couple of weeks show that he was tying together loose ends from topics he had woven throughout the letter. In the same way, this week James will cast a wide net over various circumstances we may face and will call us to put our faith to work through prayer.

To prepare for the Week 12 video, pray that God will help each person understand and apply this truth:

The prayers of the faithful are mighty. Believers should pray for one another in every circumstance—in sickness, health, suffering, and joy.

WATCH

Use the space below to take notes while you watch the Session 12 video.

1. I think the thing we miss most often is the invitation to ____________________ with the living God and to boldly approach the throne of grace.

2. You've been called to a relationship with God through Christ. That and that alone is ______________________.

3. Adopt practical ways to impede mental ______________.

4. In different times and different seasons, _____________ _______ people to pray with.

5. Mingle praise, confession, and intercession, and tie as much of it as you can back to the ______________________.

6. ____________________ digs deep roots.

7. Singing ______________ others up.

8. Singing ____________________ you for trials.

9. Dark nights of the soul are made bearable by _____________ and by singing to the Lord.

10. The Lord has designed us as _______________ people. The spirit can affect the physical and the mental.

11. The only way to ____________ darkness is to drag it into the light.

ANSWERS: 1) commune; 2) Christianity; 3) drift; 4) seek out; 5) Scriptures; 6) Singing; 7) builds; 8) strengthens; 9) worship; 10) whole; 11) kill

DISCUSS

Use the following questions to guide your discussion of the video.

Matt began his teaching from Mark 14:26-31,66-68 with a conversation between Peter and Jesus.

How would you summarize this account? What makes it a helpful backdrop for today's text in James 5:13-18?

How does Peter's life illustrate "progress, not perfection"? What does this phrase mean?

Is anyone among you suffering? Let him pray. Is anyone cheerful? Let him sing praise. Is anyone among you sick? Let him call for the elders of the church, and let them pray over him, anointing him with oil in the name of the Lord.
JAMES 5:13-14

What circumstances or seasons of life do these verses mention? How does this teaching relate to the ongoing process of faith and works in the Christian life?

What are prayer and praise? In what ways are they fundamentally the same? What place do they have in believers' spiritual growth?

We're called over and over to pray and praise. How does seeing this as a relational invitation rather than a religious obligation affect your understanding of each?

And the prayer of faith will save the one who is sick, and the Lord will raise him up. And if he has committed sins, he will be forgiven. Therefore, confess your sins to one another and pray for one another, that you may be healed. The prayer of a righteous person has great power as it is working. Elijah was a man with a nature like ours, and he prayed fervently that it might not rain, and for three years and six months it did not rain on the earth. Then he prayed again, and heaven gave rain, and the earth bore its fruit.

JAMES 5:15-18

What examples did James give to demonstrate the power of prayer in the life of a faithful believer?

Why do you think prayer is often a difficult habit, even for people who believe in the power of prayer and the presence of a loving Heavenly Father?

Matt shared seven practical tips from D. A. Carson for making progress toward a faithful prayer life.

What does each of the following tips mean? How is each one helpful?

1. Prayer needs to be planned.
2. Adopt a practical way to stop mental drift.
3. In different times and different seasons, seek out people to pray with.
4. Get around people who pray.
5. Develop a system for your prayer lists.
6. Mingle praise, confession, and intercession and tie as much of it as you can to the Scriptures.
7. Pray until you pray.[1]

Were any of these brand-new ideas for you?

What practices have you found effective for developing faithfulness and focus in your prayer life?

What remaining questions or comments do you have about the video teaching or discussion?

What was challenging, convicting, encouraging, or timely for your current circumstances?

Close in prayer.

PRAYER REQUESTS

1. Adapted from D. A. Carson, *A Call to Spiritual Reformation* (Grand Rapids, MI: Baker Academic, 1992), 19–37.

PERSONAL STUDY

PART 1: FAITHFUL

Faithfulness is about progress, not perfection.

James constantly points us to the fact that the Christian life is about glad-hearted obedience. After all the practical application of spiritual truth James addressed for five chapters, he started to close his letter with a call to prayer.

We've done the same thing throughout this book. At the end of each day's personal study, you found instructions to pray about the ongoing application and expression of your faith. You were prompted to respond to what you read and to ask God to continue working in your heart so that your actions would increasingly bear the fruit of faithfulness and righteousness.

Prayer is infinitely more than a transition in our lives from our everyday routines to a spiritual moment and then back again. Prayer is ongoing communion with God.

If God is the source of our life, salvation, hope, and righteousness—and He is—then prayer is our way of approaching Him in complete dependence and satisfaction. James repeatedly pointed out that knowing the right things about God isn't the same as a faithful life in relationship with God.

Paul put it this way:

> *My beloved, as you have always obeyed, so now, not only as in my presence but much more in my absence, work out your own salvation with fear and trembling, for it is God who works in you, both to will and to work for his good pleasure.*
> **PHILIPPIANS 2:12-13**

What did Paul mean when he wrote that God "works in you, both to will and to work for his good pleasure" (v. 13)?

Why is it significant that Paul said to work *out*, not work *for*, your own salvation?

How does the language of working out imply a process—progress, not perfection?

The letters of Paul and James push us into a beautiful tension in which faith, works, God's activity, and our activity all move together. We work, yet it's simultaneously God's work in and through us. In the Christian life, we continually move closer to God. As God works in our hearts, our salvation is worked out in our lives. Spiritual maturity is increasing dependence on God, not independence from Him. We never arrive at a point where we don't need God. We grow increasingly aware of our need for Him. And we grow to find joy in that reality.

Faithfulness requires letting go of the illusion that we can be self-sovereign. It's having our eyes opened to areas in our lives where we're still white-knuckled and clinging to control so that we can let them go, fully surrendering them to the Lord.

Jesus described this life of faithfulness—true saving faith—this way:

> *If anyone would come after me, let him deny himself and take up his cross daily and follow me. For whoever would save his life will lose it, but whoever loses his life for my sake will save it.*
> LUKE 9:23-24

Underline in these verses any words or phrases that relate to faithfulness. How would you describe the role of ongoing faithfulness in a personal relationship with Jesus?

Faith works. James' entire letter has been an exhortation to live faithfully as followers of Jesus. From beginning to end, he insisted that the Christian life puts into action our belief in God's sovereign power and goodness.

What did James teach about faithfulness—living by faith and wisdom—in the following verses?

James 1:5-8

James 1:22-27

James 2:14-26

James 3:13-18

James 4:6-10

James 5:13-18

How would you summarize James' overall teaching on faithfulness?

Ask God to increase your faith as you respond to Him in love and obedience. Give Him all glory and praise as He powerfully works through answered prayer.

PART 2: FAITHLESS

Life is tough, and it's been that way ever since the day Adam and Eve questioned God's sovereign goodness and acted unfaithfully. Everything was broken in Genesis 3. This single act of faithlessness fractured all of creation.

Paul said all of creation longs for restoration and for the curse of sin to be reversed. Everything painfully groans in the bondage of corruption (Rom. 8:19-23). Paul referred to this broken state of existence as futility (v. 20).

But God, in His faithfulness to us, wouldn't leave us in this hopeless, faithless state of futility under the curse of sin and death:

God shows his love for us in that while we were still sinners, Christ died for us.
ROMANS 5:8

And not only did Christ die for us, but the Holy Spirit also works within us:

The Spirit helps us in our weakness. For we do not know what to pray for as we ought, but the Spirit himself intercedes for us with groanings too deep for words. And he who searches hearts knows what is the mind of the Spirit, because the Spirit intercedes for the saints according to the will of God. And we know that for those who love God all things work together for good, for those who are called according to his purpose. For those whom he foreknew he also predestined to be conformed to the image of his Son, in order that he might be the firstborn among many brothers. And those whom he predestined he also called, and those whom he called he also justified, and those whom he justified he also glorified.
ROMANS 8:26-30

Summarize God's work in moving us from faithlessness to faithfulness.

Justification is a term that means we've been made right with God. Justice has been served. Jesus paid in full the debt for our sin. We're justified through faith.

Sanctification is a term that describes the ongoing process of growing in faithfulness. The Spirit of God is constantly at work conforming us to the image of Christ. Justification happens in an instant when the Father adopts us. Sanctification takes a lifetime as children of God grow to maturity.

Remember: Faithfulness is about progress, not perfection.

The first step in justification is recognizing your sin, confessing it, and repenting of it. The next steps in sanctification are also recognizing your sin, confessing it, and repenting of it. The Christian life is an ongoing ethic of confession and repentance.

Ask the Holy Spirit to help you in your weakness right now. In what ways are you weak, struggling in your faith, and living in sin as self-sovereign rather than in obedience to God's will?

How have you seen God's faithfulness to you, even in your faithlessness, both before salvation and as a follower of Jesus?

If you live according to the flesh you will die, but if by the Spirit you put to death the deeds of the body, you will live. For all who are led by the Spirit of God are sons of God. For you did not receive the spirit of slavery to fall back into fear, but you have received the Spirit of adoption as sons, by whom we cry, "Abba! Father!" The Spirit himself bears witness with our spirit that we are children of God, and if children, then heirs—heirs of God and fellow heirs with Christ, provided we suffer with him in order that we may also be glorified with him.

ROMANS 8:13-17

How do Paul's words convict you about your faithlessness?

How do Paul's words comfort you and give you confidence in faithfulness?

Be honest with yourself. Do you believe in prayer? Do you really believe God will hear and act when you pray? Do you believe He's Abba Father? Or do you feel that you need to somehow earn His favor and blessings?

Are you so foolish? Having begun by the Spirit,
are you now being perfected by the flesh?
GALATIANS 3:3

Pretending you've got it all together as a Christian isn't faithfulness; it's faithlessness. If you had it all together, you would be sinless, and there would be no room for growth because you would already be perfect. True faithfulness is the ability to admit that you earned nothing from God and now trust that He loves you and will work all things for good. Living in your own strength rather than relying on God in prayer denies the power of God working in and through you. Faithfulness comes at the end of self-reliance. Jesus taught:

Ask, and it will be given to you; seek, and you will find; knock, and it will be opened to you. For everyone who asks receives, and the one who seeks finds, and to the one who knocks it will be opened. Or which one of you, if his son asks him for bread, will give him a stone? Or if he asks for a fish, will give him a serpent? If you then, who are evil, know how to give good gifts to your children, how much more will your Father who is in heaven give good things to those who ask him!
MATTHEW 7:7-11

Read James 5:13-18 and be honest with your Father in prayer. Ask the Holy Spirit to reveal what you may not even recognize that you need to live out your faith. Confess your sin. Believe that your good Father will give you all you need to grow in faithfulness to Him. He loves you. He's good. He's faithful.

WEEK 13

WANDERER / RESTORER

GROUP STUDY

START

Welcome everyone to the group. Take a minute to review Week 12 before starting Week 13.

Before starting new content, we'll take a few minutes to review the previous week, keeping in mind that the Christian life is one of transformation, not just information. The overarching message of James is that our faith expresses itself in our works.

FAITH. In what ways is your faith growing? What's one thing you learned through group discussion or personal study this past week?

WORKS: When did the message of James seem especially relevant this past week? How did you apply what you're learning to your daily life?

This is our final session. The Book of James concludes rather abruptly, without any closing remarks or formalities. We're left with James' final words ringing in our ears as he walks offstage, so to speak.

The backbone of James' letter is the idea that faith works. And genuine, saving faith reveals itself in the way we live. James fleshed out this theme in practical ways, and his closing words remind us of the seriousness of faith.

If you're saved, you should live like it. James ended with a call for believers to reach out to wandering believers. Calling out others to examine their faith may seem harsh, but it's actually loving and gracious. Eternity hangs in the balance, so we act for their good and God's glory.

To prepare for the Week 13 video, pray that God will help each person understand and apply this truth:

As Christians, we're our brother's or sister's keeper. We must speak truth into other people's lives and guide them back to the truth when they wander.

WATCH

Use the space below to take notes while you watch the Session 13 video.

1. Conviction should always be sweet for the believer in Christ because it's an invitation to ________________ ______________ to what God is doing in our hearts.

2. You will never stop ________________ and ________________.

3. We all ______________.

4. When we give ourselves over to sin, the heart ______________.

5. The way to win a brother back is to ______________.

ANSWERS: 1) surrender ourselves; 2) confessing, repenting; 3) wander; 4) hardens; 5) love

DISCUSS

Use the following questions to guide your discussion of the video.

For our final group discussion, we'll first touch on a few points from this week's video and then wrap up by responding to the Book of James as a whole.

My brothers, if anyone among you wanders from the truth and someone brings him back, let him know that whoever brings back a sinner from his wandering will save his soul from death and will cover a multitude of sins.
JAMES 5:19-20

In your own words, what was James saying at the conclusion of his letter?

Why is this a fitting end to James' teaching on faith and works?

When have you wandered from true wisdom and godliness? How did someone help you turn back to the truth?

What questions or comments do you have about today's video teaching?

What was challenging, convicting, encouraging, or timely for your current circumstances?

In Week 1 Matt highlighted three major themes that would run throughout our study of James:

1. Trials, suffering, and difficulty can be expected. They never surprise God.
2. God desires progress, not perfection, as we follow Jesus.
3. Riches and comfort will never satisfy the soul.

What specific teachings from the Book of James can you remember about each of those three themes?

How would you summarize the primary message of James?

During the past thirteen weeks of this study, how have you responded to those three themes and to the idea of faith that works?

As stated in Week 1, our goal was to help you move closer to being fully alive in Christ by the end of this journey through the Book of James.

On a scale of 1 to 10, with 1 being spiritually dead and 10 being fully alive in joyful obedience, how would you rate your current walk with Jesus? Explain your rating.

1 2 3 4 5 6 7 8 9 10
Spiritually dead **Fully alive**

Remember that progress, not perfection, is James' message on faith and works. Sanctification is an ongoing work of the Holy Spirit in your life, conforming you to the image of Jesus.

How has this study of James changed the way you live out your faith?

What would you share with someone else about studying the Book of James?

Before ending your time together, discuss plans for your next group study.

Encourage everyone to conclude this study by completing the final week of personal study.

Close in prayer.

PRAYER REQUESTS

PERSONAL STUDY

PART 1: WANDERER

My brothers, if anyone among you wanders from the truth and someone brings him back, let him know that whoever brings back a sinner from his wandering will save his soul from death and will cover a multitude of sins.
JAMES 5:19-20

Progress, not perfection. The journey of sanctification and spiritual maturity is a lifelong process of growth. Along that journey you'll experience mistakes, failures, frustrations, and imperfections. We start lost, and we're prone to wander.

Wandering, in the context of the Book of James, refers to any intentional or unintentional departure from the truth of the gospel in word or in deed. The type of behavior James addressed happens without our noticing. This is why we need our brothers and sisters in Christ. James calls them to bring us back the way a shepherd brings back a sheep.

The prophet Isaiah compared us to sheep—a common biblical image for God's people. This isn't a term for people in general. These are God's people, His chosen and beloved people. We're dumb, helpless, wandering sheep:

All we like sheep have gone astray;
we have turned—every one—to his own way;
and the LORD has laid on him
the iniquity of us all.
ISAIAH 53:6

Circle the words *all* and *every one* in the verse.

In what ways is this verse both convicting and comforting?

The Gospel of Luke includes three consecutive parables in which Jesus illustrated the human reality of lostness and wandering.

Read Luke 15:1-7. Why did Jesus tell this parable?

What similarities do you see between Jesus' parable of the lost sheep and James 5:19-20?

Read Luke 15:8-10. What does the parable of the lost coin say about the nature of people and the nature of God?

Read Luke 15:11-32. What happened in your life to help you recognize the futility of life apart from God the Father?

Do you relate to the son who wandered into the sin of self-indulgence or to the son who wandered into the sin of self-righteousness? Why?

What's the response in all three parables to the restoration of what was lost? How should this response motivate you to view God and others?

The hymn "Come, Thou Fount of Every Blessing" expresses a powerful confession you'll probably identify with. More than 250 years after it was written, the words ring just as true and as desperate today:

O to grace how great a debtor daily I'm constrained to be!
Let Thy grace, Lord, like a fetter, bind my wand'ring heart to Thee:
Prone to wander, Lord, I feel it, prone to leave the God I love;
Here's my heart, Lord, take and seal it; seal it for Thy courts above.[1]

The hymn writer knew he couldn't trust himself. Knowing his heart was wicked and sinful, he said he would be better off bound to God by a fetter—like an ungrateful servant chained to his good master.

Nobody lies as well to you as you do:

The heart is deceitful above all things,
and desperately sick;
who can understand it?
JEREMIAH 17:9

We're completely dependent on God's grace to save us from ourselves. Following Christ requires taking up our cross daily (Luke 9:23) and dying to our desire to be self-sovereign. Whether our wandering is self-indulgent worldliness or self-righteous arrogance, our Father freely offers His goodness and grace to the prodigal who returns. His loving embrace welcomes us home.

In what ways are you wandering from the truth? In what ways are others you know wandering from the truth?

Conclude your time of personal study by meditating on Isaiah 53. Allow yourself to feel the weight of sin and wandering from the truth.

Confess your tendency to be spiritually sidetracked, to allow your affections to wander selfishly to the things of this world. Confess your lack of concern for the salvation and spiritual health of others around you. Pray for compassion and courage to share the joy of heaven that comes to those who repent of their sin.

1. Robert Robinson, "Come, Thou Fount of Every Blessing," *Baptist Hymnal* (Nashville: LifeWay Worship, 2008), 98.

PART 2: RESTORER

Confess your sins to one another and pray for one another, that you may be healed. The prayer of a righteous person has great power as it is working.
JAMES 5:16

Restoration begins with confession. You can't fix what you don't recognize is broken.

James' letter doesn't wrap up with final words of greeting like most of Paul's letters. James didn't close by naming particular individuals or by offering a broad theological statement of praise. Instead, he hammered home one final practical application of faith in action. If someone isn't putting their faith into action, call them out and point them back in the right direction:

My brothers, if anyone among you wanders from the truth and someone brings him back, let him know that whoever brings back a sinner from his wandering will save his soul from death and will cover a multitude of sins.
JAMES 5:19-20

What a great note to end on. It rings in our ears with force and finality.

Salvation from sin and death is the result of true, saving faith in Jesus. Faith works. It's active. It's selfless. It bears fruit. At times our active faith will call us to pursue the failing faith of another person. Jesus outlined a process for doing so:

If your brother sins against you, go and tell him his fault, between you and him alone. If he listens to you, you have gained your brother. But if he does not listen, take one or two others along with you, that every charge may be established by the evidence of two or three witnesses. If he refuses to listen to them, tell it to the church. And if he refuses to listen even to the church, let him be to you as a Gentile and a tax collector.
MATTHEW 18:15-17

Have you ever pursued a person who was wandering from the truth? What was that process like? How did he or she respond?

Why is such a process necessary, even though it may make us feel uncomfortable?

Why did God give the church the unique responsibility to pursue people who wander from the truth?

Wandering from the truth means we're pursuing something less than God's best for us in the gospel. This is a matter of life and death. This is why Jesus outlined a process to reconcile wanders from the truth. While the process is often known as church discipline, the goal isn't punishment but reconciliation. We pursue wanderers, hoping they'll return to the truth and be reconciled to God and the community of the church. Because God reconciled us to Himself at the cross, we help others find the same reconciliation we've found.

Paul put it this way:

> *If anyone is in Christ, he is a new creation. The old has passed away; behold, the new has come. All this is from God, who through Christ reconciled us to himself and gave us the ministry of reconciliation; that is, in Christ God was reconciling the world to himself, not counting their trespasses against them, and entrusting to us the message of reconciliation.*
>
> **2 CORINTHIANS 5:17-19**

James, the half brother of Jesus, was convinced and forever changed by the life, death, and resurrection of Christ. He wrote the letter you've studied so that you'll continue the ministry of reconciliation

How does pursuing and restoring those who wander echo the heart of God?

How did God restore you when you wandered from the truth? How does He continue to do so today?

God is a God of pursuit. In the garden He looked for Adam and Eve after they sinned and called out to them as they tried to hide in shame (Gen. 3:8-9). When sin infected the whole world, God came in the flesh—Immanuel, God with us (Matt. 1:23). And in the end He will come again to restore all things and bring about the completion of His redemptive plan:

> *I saw a new heaven and a new earth, for the first heaven and the first earth had passed away, and the sea was no more. And I saw the holy city, new Jerusalem, coming down out of heaven from God, prepared as a bride adorned for her husband. And I heard a loud voice from the throne saying, "Behold, the dwelling place of God is with man. He will dwell with them, and they will be his people, and God himself will be with them as their God. He will wipe away every tear from their eyes, and death shall be no more, neither shall there be mourning, nor crying, nor pain anymore, for the former things have passed away." And he who was seated on the throne said, "Behold, I am making all things new." Also he said, "Write this down, for these words are trustworthy and true." And he said to me, "It is done! I am the Alpha and the Omega, the beginning and the end. To the thirsty I will give from the spring of the water of life without payment.*
>
> REVELATION 21:1-6

Conclude your study of the Book of James by praising God for salvation and restoration. Thank Jesus for covering your sins with the blood He shed on the cross. Thank Him for the new life made possible through His resurrection. Meditate on the glory of eternal life in His presence, when all things will be made new and fully restored.

LEADER GUIDE

1. PRAYERFULLY PREPARE

Prepare for each group session with prayer. Ask the Holy Spirit to work through you and the group discussion as you point to Jesus each week through God's Word.

2. ENCOURAGE DISCUSSION

A good small-group experience has the following characteristics.

EVERYONE PARTICIPATES. Encourage everyone to ask questions, share responses, or read aloud.

NO ONE DOMINATES—NOT EVEN THE LEADER. Be sure your time speaking as a leader takes up less than half your time together as a group. Politely guide discussion if anyone dominates.

DON'T RUSH THROUGH QUESTIONS. Don't feel that a moment of silence is a bad thing. Students often need time to think about their responses to questions they've just heard or to gain courage to share what God is stirring in their hearts.

AFFIRM AND FOLLOW UP ON INPUT. Make sure you point out something true or helpful in a response. Don't just move on. Build community with follow-up questions, asking how others have experienced similar things or how a truth has shaped their understanding of God and the Scripture you're studying.

KEEP GOD AND HIS WORD CENTRAL. Opinions and experiences can be helpful, but God has given us the truth. Trust Scripture to be the authority and God's Spirit to work in people's lives. You can't change anyone, but God can. Continually point people to the Word and to active steps of faith.

3. KEEP CONNECTING

Think of ways to connect with group members during the week. Participation during the group session is always improved when members spend time connecting with one another outside the group sessions. The more students are comfortable with one another and involved in one another's lives, the more they'll look forward to being together.

Encourage group members with thoughts, commitments, or questions from the session by connecting through emails, texts, and social media. Build deeper friendships by planning or spontaneously inviting group members to join you outside your regularly scheduled group time for meals; fun activities; and projects around your school, church, or community.

4. LEADING THE SESSIONS

Thank you for being willing to lead a group through an in-depth examination of the Book of James. If this is your first time leading a group, don't overthink it. Prepare to lead by viewing the video session, reading the suggestions for the group session, and completing the personal study each week. Be prepared to distribute Bible-study books and to show each video session. For Week 1 you'll want to familiarize group members with the format of the study, including the way the group session will be structured ("Start," "Watch," "Discuss") and the features of the Bible-study book (two personal studies each week). In addition, use the following guides to help you prepare for the group sessions.

WEEK 1

Week 1 will introduce the Book of James. Emphasize the personal nature of our faith. Nobody can believe or obey God on our behalf. Each person has to submit to the authority of Jesus as Lord. A relationship with Jesus through faith will change our identity and therefore our activity since behavior flows from identity.

Before concluding, explain that each time the group meets, you'll start the session by reviewing the previous week's topic. Your review will follow a major theme from the Book of James: faith and works. Emphasize the importance of reading and applying Scripture throughout the week, especially since James' point is that knowing truth about God doesn't matter if we don't live in faithful obedience.

NOTES

WEEK 2

Beginning this week, you'll start each group session by reviewing the previous week's study. This is an important time of accountability and encouragement. Evaluate the time you've allotted for the session and aim to manage that time well, allowing time to start with the review and to discuss the teaching after the video.

This week will discuss trials and temptation. Don't let the group session become a time to dwell on personal opinions or to vent about individual circumstances. Although you want to develop honesty and trust among group members, the primary goal of this session should be a firm conviction that God is good and trustworthy.

NOTES

WEEK 3

At this point students should start getting comfortable with the routine, including the time of review at the start of the session. Don't omit this review. This week James starts hitting his stride, introducing the heart behind his letter: it's not enough to hear the truth; we must do what it says. Emphasize the similarities in James' writing to Jesus' teaching, especially the Sermon on the Mount. Encourage students to put into practice what they're studying and discussing each week from God's Word.

NOTES

WEEK 4

Throughout his letter James goes back and forth between general principles of the Christian life and specific issues in the church. This is a prime example of Christians who didn't put into practice what they had been taught. Point out that we're all likely to be self-serving sometimes, even as Christians. Encourage group members not to beat themselves up over sin but to recognize it for what it is. The Christian life is one of continual growth and maturity. Emphasize that all of our behavior ultimately flows from our identity in Christ and our relationship with our good Heavenly Father.

NOTES

WEEK 5

This week's topic is the heart of James' letter: faith and works. Remind people of James' style of weaving back and forth between themes. Today he returns to the doing theme introduced in Week 3. James points to the work of loving others as evidence of our faith and true love for God, as he did at the end of chapter 1 with his definition of pure and undefiled religion. Emphasize that James isn't saying we earn our salvation or add to our faith but rather our faith is revealed by our works. Evidence and earning are opposites in respect to faith.

NOTES

WEEK 6

This week focuses on a behavior that's arguably the area of greatest weakness for most believers. Although Christians aren't perfect, we're making progress, and our speech is a good indicator of where we are in our spiritual growth. Emphasize the broad nature of sinful, unhealthy speech; it's more than just cursing someone. Don't let people dismiss unhealthy speech as inevitable by saying, "Nobody's perfect." Stress that words carry great power to hurt and heal. Help group members see how even areas of sin in their speech can be turned into good opportunities to deal with heart issues.

NOTES

WEEK 7

The midway point is a good time to evaluate the learning process. You may want to ask group members how they're doing with their personal studies and practical application of faith and works.

This week reframes the concept of hearing and doing as a worldview that will be explored in the next two sessions. Ultimately, the way we see life and make decisions is the practical expression of faith and works. What we value and believe determines what we do.

NOTES

WEEK 8

Week 8 continues to examine two contradictory worldviews introduced last week. Acting on true wisdom will lead to growth in godliness. Living according to false wisdom will result in worldliness. Point out that James is once again restating the idea that what we truly believe and what we do are inseparable.

NOTES

WEEK 9

This week James returns to a practical example of the broader truth he explored in previous verses. Point out how a posture of arrogance or humility is rooted in a worldly or godly perspective. Clarify that plans are a sign of wisdom, but the motivation behind those plans reveals whether we're acting from a heart of faith. Help students see the progressive nature of James' teaching and ways their beliefs affect every part of their lives.

NOTES

WEEK 10

If you haven't already done so, decide what you'll study after you finish Week 13 of *James: Faith/Works.* As the leader, you may have noticed some questions or themes during the discussions over the past nine weeks which may require further study as a group. You may want to suggest options, request ideas, or simply communicate your plans for what's next. If you're providing books for the next study, get a final count of participants so you can purchase books to distribute in Week 13.

This week James continues to address a specific area of sin. Don't be afraid of the strong language he uses to condemn a posture of arrogance and abuse for the sake of personal gain. Familiarize yourself with other Scriptures that address money, especially Paul's teaching in 1 Timothy 6:6-10 and Jesus' teaching in Matthew 6:19-34. Clarify that money isn't inherently sinful. God has blessed us through common grace, but the Bible teaches throughout that money is dangerous.

NOTES

WEEK 11

James returns to his message of hope and endurance he introduced in chapter 1. One of the greatest temptations Christians face is to doubt God's goodness of God in the midst of difficulty, especially if it's caused by others who claim the name of Jesus. Point out how James encourages those who are suffering to keep their faith focused on the reality of Jesus and the hope of the gospel.

By this point in the study, some level of trust and comfort should be established. This session deals with the forgiveness of sin and provides a natural opportunity to be honest with one another about salvation in Jesus Christ. Be prepared to lead a time of prayer for your group. Encourage group members through personal testimony and the Word of God.

NOTES

WEEK 12

You have only two group sessions remaining, including this one. Finalize any future plans. You'll want to decide what to study next to ensure you have time to order books.

In this week's study, James emphasizes the necessity of prayer. Point out that prayer is the ultimate expression of faith at work. Remind group members that biblical commands are an invitation to something greater. Emphasize the sufficiency and all-satisfying nature of our Heavenly Father.

NOTES

WEEK 13

In this final week's study, leave plenty of time to reflect on and review the entire study. This is an important part of processing and applying what everyone has learned. Discussion of what has been most meaningful to people is often a rich time of encouragement and honesty. Pay attention to what people say, because their comments will give you great insight into their need for further spiritual growth or into their readiness to take next steps in leadership.

Communicate plans for when and where you'll meet next and what you'll study. Distribute any Bible-study books you may have purchased for group members or be sure they know how to get their own books before the next study begins.

NOTES